Integrated Planning for Campus Information Systems:

A Series of Conferences for Undergraduate Institutions Sponsored by OCLC and the Association of American Colleges

OCLC Library, Information, and Computer Science Series

Integrated Planning for Campus Information Systems:

A Series of Conferences for Undergraduate Institutions Sponsored by OCLC and the Association of American Colleges

Edited by Daphne N. Layton

OCLC Online Computer Library Center, Inc.
6565 Frantz Road
Dublin, Ohio 43017-0702

© 1989 OCLC Online Computer Library Center, Inc.
6565 Frantz Road
Dublin, Ohio 43017-0702

Printed in the United States of America

ISBN: 1-55653-071-4
       0-933418-35-3 (series)

1   2   3   4   5 | 92   91   90   89

The paper used in this publication meets the minimum requirements of American National Standard for Information Science—Permanence of Paper for Printed Library Materials, ANSI Z39.48-1984.

∞ ™

Library of Congress Cataloging-in-Publication Data

Integrated planning for campus information systems.

(OCLC library, information, and computer science series ; 12)
1. Universities and colleges–United States–Data processing–Congresses. 2. Educational technology–United States–Congresses. I. Layton, Daphne Niobe, 1961-   . II. OCLC. III. Association of American Colleges. IV. Series.
LB2341.I546   1989   378.1'0285   89-8732
ISBN 1-55653-071-4

Contents

Preface

The papers in this publication resulted from a series of three conferences sponsored jointly by the OCLC Online Computer Library Center and the Association of American Colleges (AAC) to discuss integrated planning for campus information systems. The conferences themselves were extraordinarily successful, and this volume represents an effort to share the benefits that the participants received.

Computers made a cautious appearance on most college and university campuses some twenty-five years ago. Since then they have had a revolutionary impact upon many areas of college life: teaching, research, business processes, and the storage and retrieval of information. As information technology continues to evolve rapidly, so do the applications. The pace of change in both the technology and its applications poses difficult challenges for college and university officers who must make decisions that often entail large monetary expenditures and the reorganization of the working relationships among various campus operations. Libraries in particular have been affected by the new information technology, with the result that they are able to respond much more rapidly and more voluminously to the needs of users.

The papers in this volume are designed to help campus decision makers understand better the reshaping of campus information systems by the new technology. Equipped with this improved understanding, these decision makers should be better prepared to make wise choices in this critically important area of college and university operations.

Rowland C. W. Brown
Former President
OCLC Online Computer
Library Center, Inc.

John W. Chandler
President
Association of American Colleges

Acknowledgments

I would be remiss if I did not take this opportunity to acknowledge the contributions of several people to the success of the conferences. OCLC's critical role is described in the Introduction, but Pat Barkey and Paul Schrank deserve special thanks for their persevering hard work, especially during the early stages. OCLC also has our gratitude for publishing these proceedings, which was overseen by Philip Schieber.

AAC and OCLC are greatly indebted to the presenters for the generosity and enthusiasm with which they relinquished precious time to our conferences far in excess of typical demands. Their additional work in preparing these papers is also appreciated.

The members of the advisory committee to the project, Deanna Marcum, James Powell, and JoAn Segal, were thoughtful, helpful, and generous with their time and advice. We couldn't have done it without them.

At AAC, Joseph Johnston and Shelagh Casey were in the trenches from the beginning. As Director of Programs, Joe was a source of guidance in every phase of conference conceptualization, planning, and execution. Shelagh made sure every conference ran smoothly, and when I left AAC in December of 1987, she took over my role as principal director of the project. Nora Topalian assisted with many administrative details throughout the project's duration.

Finally, it is the Andrew W. Mellon Foundation that made it all possible and gave AAC the flexibility and encouragement to move into a new and difficult area with confidence.

Daphne N. Layton

Introduction

Daphne N. Layton

Increasing in quantity at a dizzying rate, information and the technology used to process it offer unique opportunities to institutions of higher learning. Electronic publishing allows scholars and researchers to consult the work of colleagues far more quickly than traditional book publishing allows. Online catalogs allow sophisticated searches to enormous databases—searches that might have taken hours, if they were even feasible—to be completed within seconds. Networks make possible the communication of students and faculty over large distances, the transfer of data from large mainframe computers to individual personal computers, and the replacement of crowded, immobile computer centers with systems in which every student and faculty member on a campus has his or her own terminal.

As inviting as these prospects appear, they pose difficult questions for individual colleges and universities. Quite apart from the

Daphne N. Layton is a doctoral candidate in Administration, Planning, and Social Policy, Harvard Graduate School of Education, and former Assistant Director of Programs, Association of American Colleges.

problem of applying limited resources to expensive new technology, technological advances are forcing the college community to confront challenges ranging from rethinking the role of a central campus institution—the library—to restructuring the tenure evaluation process.

Furthermore, most institutions have had enough experience with technology to question the high expectations that have been raised about technology's benefits for education. A higher education computer consultant recently quoted one college president as saying, "Somebody promised me that computers and technology would make my institution more productive, easier to manage, and more sophisticated educationally. None of these things has happened."[1] As the consultant later concluded, technology has to contribute to the mission of an institution, and not just make it more expensive to run.

One of the most obvious, and difficult, tasks for those involved in deciding an institution's technological future is that of relating these changes and advances to the college's educational goals. What kind of information technology, at what level of integration, can best allow the library, media services, and the academic computer center to support instruction and research—the central functions of a college or university? Will technology be used to improve the way colleges do what they have always done, or will it occasion a fundamental shift in goals? Should the information technology on a campus be integrated (into a campus information system)? To what extent? What implications does integration have for the campus budgeting and decision-making processing—in other words, for organizational planning?

There is now widespread agreement that advanced information technology is here to stay on American campuses, large and small. To ignore the opportunities afforded by technology at short-term savings is to severely compromise an institution's competitiveness in the future. As William Beeman indicates in his paper, students are increasingly entering college with significant amounts of experience in computing. They will expect opportunities to continue learning and using these tools during their undergraduate years. Furthermore, today's students will be using technology more and more during their adult lives as productive citizens. In fulfilling their missions of preparing students for those lives, colleges need to pay attention to this changing reality. Faculty will also begin to expect sophisticated information resources for their teaching and research activities. Already, the existence—or absence—of attractive technological facilities is playing a role in the ability of institutions to hire the faculty they want.

Clearly, technology represents an investment that has to be made, and has to be made sooner rather than later. While the MITs and Vanderbilts of the world—the large research universities—have resources and incentives for becoming technological pioneers, most institutions, especially smaller ones, cannot afford to be this bold. As James Emery says,

> Not all institutions view computing with equal favor or have resources to keep up with leaders in the field. A few will reap tremendous strategic benefits from building reputations as leaders in technology. For the typical institution, a more realistic alternative is to position [itself] as either an aggressive or casual follower. Letting others do the pioneering and then picking up the fruits of their efforts at a relatively low cost makes a great deal of sense, even if it means forgoing the substantial (but probably unattainable) advantage of being recognized as a leader in the field . . . an inability to stay at the forefront of technology should not be used as an excuse for inaction.[2]

Institutions oriented primarily toward teaching undergraduates will not—and cannot—make the same choices as large research universities. But they do have to find the right level of technology for their campuses and move sooner rather than later to implement a campus information system. In some cases, this may require overcoming substantial resistance among members of the collegiate community toward the intrusion of potentially "dehumanizing" technology and all its wordly implications into the ivied centers of reflection and learning. But such resistance is becoming rare. While some faculty and administrators might have difficulty thinking of small liberal arts colleges as "wired," the fact is that there is no dichotomy between a mission of liberal education and the tools for learning and processing information that are offered by technology. As Richard Detweiler, who describes his institution as "militantly liberal arts," says in his paper that appears in this volume, "we now have a revolutionary opportunity in liberal education—the opportunity to use technology to increase the access to and use of knowledge and thereby counteract the narrowness forced on us in recent years by the abundance of information . . . Computer technology is a tool for liberal education."

Campus Information System

What is a campus information system? It is a system for storing, processing, providing access to, and communicating information and knowledge to those who seek it (students, faculty, and staff). In earlier times, this system may have consisted of pen, paper, and mailbox. Today, the phrase "campus information system" can mean many different things, but it often includes these elements: mainframe, mini- or microcomputer systems on campus for academic and administrative uses, often able to communicate with each other; automated library functions such as an online catalog, automated circulation, and online searching of remote databases; and a network or networks allowing voice, data and/or video communication between different computers on and off campus. These systems vary from the relatively straightforward to the exceedingly complex. The important thing to remember is that no matter what its elements—and these will change over time—the system needs to be conceived and evaluated in terms of the educational goals it is serving.

A campus information system is human as well as technological. In some ways, the available technologies and their capabilities of interaction and integration have progressed far more rapidly than the ability of campus decision-makers to make the administrative and organizational changes needed to accommodate the new ways that information is provided and processed on a campus. As one observer has noted, "this new way of life has outpaced our efforts to conceptualize, develop, and finance the new infrastructure necessary for the full and productive use of the new technologies."[3] These efforts, however, are critical to the success of a campus information system. As perplexing as the hardware problems might be, the necessity of rethinking organizational structures is proving even more challenging for many institutions. Many are finding it desirable to create new positions of administrative responsibility for technological functions across the boundaries of traditionally separate entities such as the library, academic computing, and administrative computing.

It is precisely because of the structural implications of adopting information technology on campus that the issues need to be addressed on an institutionwide basis. The boundaries between organizational, technological, and educational aspects of computing are blurred and always changing. Integrated planning must involve those with responsibility for each of these dimensions. It must occur on an organizational level as much as on a technological level. For economic reasons as much as any others, things such as "evaluation and selection of hardware and software, setting of technical standards, and provision of high-tech support services are usually best handled at the institutional level,"[4] not to mention establishing mechanisms for using a common campus network, supporting common workstations, and providing access to common databases.

Many institutions have already made substantial inroads in planning for or implementing aspects of a campus information system. Yet, to a large extent, and especially among those institutions that are not in the top tier of pioneering research universities, each campus is approaching this challenge on its own. Few individuals claim established expertise in this area—something we began to refer to in the office as the "new modesty" of higher education consultants—and those with experience relevant to smaller or undergraduate institutions are even more rare. The enormity of the implications of technological decisions for campuses of this type makes this relative isolation not only unfortunate but deleterious.

It was with all of these concerns in mind that in late 1986 Paul Schrank and Pat Barkey of OCLC Online Computer Library Center initiated a series of conversations with the Association of American Colleges (AAC) that resulted in the conferences at which the following papers were presented. OCLC is best known for the OCLC Online Union Catalog, the largest database of library bibliographic information in the world, containing 16 million records in 1987. More than 7,900 libraries contribute to and/or use the catalog. OCLC also provides numerous other technology-oriented services to its members.

Paul and Pat expressed a desire to get a better idea of the concerns of smaller, primarily teaching-oriented institutions in the area of advanced technology, not only for the library. At the same time, AAC, an organization whose mission is to help improve and advance undergraduate education, was aware that increasingly the shape of higher education in every kind of institution will be influenced by information technology in ways few people anticipated even twenty years ago. The interest evinced by OCLC coincided perfectly with AAC's wish to undertake work in this complex arena.

Working closely with OCLC, we designed a series of small conferences for AAC-member colleges and universities, one in Washington, D.C., in June 1987; one in Columbus, Ohio, in November 1987; and one in Pomona, California, in February 1988. The conferences were funded by a grant from the Andrew W. Mellon Foundation. The only cost to participating institutions was travel to and from the meeting for five representatives.

Our target for the conferences was institutions whose primary orientation is undergraduate teaching and who had made some progress in planning or implementing a campus information system or elements of one. We invited a regional cross-section of AAC members in the Carnegie categories of Liberal Arts Colleges and Comprehensive Universities to apply for admission to each conference, which was limited to eight institutions. In the end, more than sixty colleges and universities (or 12 percent of those invited) sent in applications, about half of those for the East Coast meeting. Given the difficulty of assembling the required team, this seemed to us a strong indication of both the timeliness of the issues these kinds of institutions are facing with regard to new technology and their need for outside assistance in thinking them through.

Conference Design

In several aspects, the conference design was modeled on a pioneering conference sponsored by OCLC in the summer of 1986. Called "Conference on Information Resources for the Campus of the Future,"[5] this meeting brought together officials of some of the country's leading research universities—themselves pioneers in the computer revolution in academic institutions—to discuss some of the very same issues. An important element of that conference, and one that we adopted for our meetings, was the requirement that participating institutions send a team of representatives to the meeting. The team had to include the president or chancellor of the institution.

In addition to the president, we invited the chief academic officer of the institution, the librarian, the director of academic computing or computer center director, and an interested and informed faculty member to be chosen by the rest of the team. In some instances, these five persons, whose cooperation is critical to the success of an integrated campus information system, had not previously met as a group to discuss the issues to which the conference was dedicated. Barring a last-minute emergency, no institution was allowed to participate without its president.

Eight institutions were represented at each conference. They varied in size and type from very small, rural liberal arts colleges to mid-size urban universities. However, they had in common some degree of knowledge and experience with the problems and opportunities presented by new technology for undergraduate education on their campuses. While no one institution had "done it all," almost every one had taken strides in at least one aspect of an information system—automating library circulation, establishing a sophisticated local area network, or providing elaborate PC labs on campus for students, for instance. Descriptions of the technological environments of the participating institutions may be found in appendix B.

Each meeting lasted for approximately one-and-a-half days. There were six formal presenters, all of whom stayed for the duration of all three conferences, with the exception of one, whose presentation was videotaped in Columbus so that she could be "with us" in Pomona. The sessions included lecture-style presentations by three of the speakers and a panel session involving the other three.

Presentations

We were fortunate in having with us presenters who understood the particular challenges being faced by these groups of institutions, even if they themselves did not hail primarily from that kind of environment. **William Beeman** addresses his remarks to the need for assessment and evaluation of computing and technology on campus, with special attention to educational applications. Although his laboratory is Brown University, his points have clear relevance for all institutions. He argues that technological decisions, especially those affecting scholarship and education, must be informed by accurate and sensible data on the behavior of students and faculty with regard to technology. If such research is not undertaken, the risk of waste and lost opportunities is too high.

Richard Boss devotes his attention to a discussion of library automation options, both technical and administrative. He describes some of the benefits and pitfalls of library technology and sums up with practical advice for institutions of any size. Someone who has been described as having set foot in more academic libraries than anyone else in the country, Mr. Boss was a key resource during the conference for both librarians and administrators who were struggling with myriad questions regarding the automation of their libraries.

As an example of one undergraduate institution's path-breaking use of technology, **Richard Detweiler** discusses Drew University's Computer Initiative, in which personal computers have been given to all students, faculty, and staff at the university. Dr. Detweiler comments on the role of computer technology in liberal education and discusses at length the administrative changes that accompanied the implementation of the Computer Initiative at Drew. Whether or not an institution adopts the particular plan that Drew has worked out, Dr. Detweiler's discussion of organizational planning should be of keen interest to faculty and administrators alike.

In a relaxed after-dinner address, **Evan Farber** called attention to the implications of technology for teaching and learning, with special reference to the changing role of the library. Mr. Farber discussed the processes of learning and the role that people—teachers, librarians, and other students—will always play in it, no matter how the tools of information-gathering change. While he heralds the ongoing advances of technology as opening up untold new options for research and teaching, he cautions that we must be careful that our students do not learn to equate information with knowledge. Librarians and other professionals will always be needed, he concludes, and more so now than ever, to help sort through massive quantities of information.

In his paper, **James Johnson** provides a helpful overview of technology today and tomorrow and discusses various planning-related issues. The first speaker at each of the conferences, Mr. Johnson offered a mixture of practical advice and historical background on computers, telecommunications, and other areas of technology important to the university. It was clear from the questions his presentation generated that it was of prime interest even to participants who could boast considerable knowledge about academic technology.

Finally, **Patricia Skarulis** directs her remarks to organizational and planning aspects of coordinating and implementing a successful academic information system. Ms. Skarulis offers different strategies for coping with the expense and hidden costs of academic technology as well as for approaching the changes that will be occasioned by its use in terms of governance and communication between administrative units. She stresses the importance, as does Richard Detweiler, of getting not only key decision makers but also others—notably faculty—to "sign on" and work together to make the system work.

As important as these sessions and presentations were, the overwhelming response of participants indicated that it was several other aspects of the meetings that held the most value for them.

We designed the conferences so that there would be opportunities for semistructured dialogue as well as informal conversation between three subsets of participants:

- **Participants and Presenters.** Each conference included an hour-long period during which participants, having heard the formal presentations, could circulate among the six speakers and speak with them individually or in small groups. This feature was possible due to the small overall size of each conference, which had no more than forty institutional participants.

- **Peer Groups of Participants.** We provided an opportunity in each meeting for participants to meet with their colleagues in similar positions in other institutions. There were group meetings of presidents, librarians, faculty, and so on for an hour each. These sessions were generally led informally by one of the presenters or a member of the project's advisory committee.

- **Institutional Teams.** Just before the closing luncheon of each conference, teams from each institution reconvened for a time to share their thoughts, plan follow-up meetings or activities upon their return to campus, and think about anything they wanted to contribute to a closing discussion during lunch.

There were also ample opportunities for social and less formal discussion during meals and receptions. Although there was little free time and all of the conferences were characterized by full schedules and long periods of intense concentration, most participants found the effort worthwhile. The time set aside for meeting with colleagues from other institutions and presenters was a key to the usefulness of the conference for most participants.

An additional feature that proved useful was our requirement that each president give a presentation of ten minutes' length at the beginning of the conference. The presidents used this opportunity to bring up some of the issues with which their campus was engaged and what they hoped they might gain from the meeting. This exercise served the dual purpose of forcing the chief executive officers of each campus to focus on the conference agenda well in advance of the meeting and conveying to all participants the seriousness with which their senior administrators were approaching the problems and challenges of "wiring the campus." More than one president confided to us that this requirement, though onerous in some ways, was a critical component in the subsequent value of the meeting for the institution.

I mention all of these things because they point to a number of benefits of these conferences that can be realized by institutions everywhere without the opportunity for formal conference participation enjoyed by these twenty-four colleges and universities. It would be difficult to underestimate the importance of hearing from established experts in the field of academic and library technology. However, in most cases, the greatest benefit of conference participation was the opportunity of those on campus charged with developing and implementing campus information systems or their components to have the ear of their president for two days—not only at the conference, but also while traveling to and from it. This often resulted in a new dedication of resources and interest on the part of top-level administrators. The structured opportunity for team members to discuss their campus agenda on this issue was also important. As one faculty participant later wrote,

> I am positive that [the conference] will serve to help our campus' efforts. Already we are discussing a President's committee charged with producing a master plan in this area—a direction in which I have been trying to move since my arrival here. Thank you for the added push! I found the content and the organization excellent though I feel that the greatest success of these conferences is in the forced interaction and discussion of the issues it creates within the various college teams. The presentations and discussions with other college teams serve to foster discussion and new ideas within one's own team.[6]

Participants also reported that talking with their colleagues from similar institutions grappling with the same problems was very helpful. In any one aspect of an information system, approaches taken on different campuses varied widely, providing opportunities for mutual exploration and discussion of alternatives. In many instances, the foundations of lasting relationships were established. Although these institutions were often well known to each other on other levels, few of them had explored the possibilities of cooperation or discussion with regard to technological issues and problems.

These kinds of opportunities exist on any campus and in any region. While experts will always be needed, much can be learned from neighbors and institutional cousins. Within a campus, it takes initiative and cooperation, but it is possible to convene the key actors in technological decision-making for the same kinds of discussions. Many campuses are already doing this. It is our hope that the publication of information from these three AAC/OCLC conferences on campus information systems will help stimulate similar movement on other campus throughout the country.

Endnotes

1. Quoted in Linda H. Fleit, "Overselling Technology: Suppose You Gave a Computer Revolution and Nobody Came?" *The Chronicle of Higher Education* 33(32)(April 22, 1987):96.

2. James C. Emery, "Issues in Building an Information Technology Strategy." *EDUCOM Bulletin* 19(3)(Fall 1984):8.

3. Patricia Battin, "The Electronic Scholar," *CGS Communicator* (March 1987):2.

4. Emery, 9.

5. OCLC, *Campus of the Future: Conference on Information Resources* (Dublin, Ohio: OCLC Online Computer Library Center, 1986).

6. Written evaluation of June 1987 conference.

Assessing Intensive Computing on the College Campus: A Research Summary

William O. Beeman

Introduction

The Assessment of New Technology

Higher education today faces a dilemma in trying to come to grips with the rapid pace of technological change. The information explosion begun two decades ago, first with the advent of video technology and more recently with the entry of interactive computing in education, is making demands on universities unprecedented in the history of higher education. No college administrator needs to be reminded that every new student and faculty member entering a college campus today expects to see advanced computing and information facilities available in the form of electronic library catalogs, personal computers, central electronic communications facilities, and high-quality printing. Moreover, members of the campus community increasingly expect such facilities to be made

---

William O. Beeman is Associate Director for Program Analysis, Institute for Research in Information and Scholarship (IRIS) and Associate Professor of Anthropology, Brown University.

available to them free of direct personal cost. With colleges and universities competing for an ever-more-limited pool of talented students and faculty, most colleges and universities feel the pressure to provide these facilities, even if it causes budgetary strain.

The pace of development has been so rapid that almost no work has been done to assess the effects of this technological revolution on academic life. The emphasis has been largely on hype—higher education institutions touting their latest acquisition, often without thinking much about how it is used or what effect it has on the campus users. Because of the amounts of money being spent, it would seem that assessment would be essential for all programs, but it has unfortunately not been so. In the entire nation there are not more than a half-dozen active programs of evaluation of the effects of computing in higher education.

We need to know what the money we are spending on advanced technology is doing to produce better scholarship, and we need to know how to make the technology we purchase work much better.

Useful Assessment Is Difficult

Despite the need for assessment, we lack the background knowledge necessary to carry out the process effectively. In general, one cannot assess the experience of technological change unless one first understands the nature of the community in which the change is taking place (in this case the campus) in all of its subtlety. The things likely to be affected by technology include:

1. Philosophy and goals of pedagogy and the means needed to achieve them.

2. Work routines of academic workers and how they gauge progress for themselves.

3. The nature of the scholarly use of communication in formulating and disseminating research.

4. The role of library information tools in the entire spectrum of the research process.

5. Student conceptions of academic goals and the work needed to achieve them.

In the United States, we seem unwilling to spend the time or money or effort to find these things out. There are a number of reasons for this. First, many of the phenomena, such as pedagogical goals and scholarly work routines, seem obvious to people who have lived their entire professional lives in an academic setting. In fact they are not at all obvious. A scholar knows well how he or she undertakes teaching, research and writing, but has very little notion of what his or her colleagues do to complete their research. Pedagogical philosophies are rarely discussed with any seriousness either in meetings or in print. Communication patterns on and off campus are largely taken for granted even though they may be the most important determinants of what topics get scholarly attention. Libraries are studied in a narrow sense, but studies of the role of the library in broad-spectrum campus work patterns are rare. At some campuses the library may function more as a social gathering place than as a place where scholarly research takes place. Finally, we know virtually nothing about college students and how they view their own learning processes. Since all of these dimensions of campus life are likely to change with advances in computing and other information technology, it would seem imperative for us to devote attention to obtaining data about them.

There are some understandable reasons for this lack of research. Much information about campus life, and especially about work routines on campus, is not easily quantifiable. Because these phenomena are new to scholarly inquiry, they must first be carefully described. We do not know what constitutes a quantum of research in mathematics, or what stages of writing comprise a literary treatise. But we can collaborate with mathematicians, literary scholars, and others in the academic world to help build models of the way they work.

This research is also hampered by financial limitations. Discovering basic truths about people's styles of work, communication, teaching and use of academic resources takes immense creativity, time, and money. Advertising and marketing firms spend large amounts of money and effort discovering similar information to bring about changes in public buying habits, but despite their efforts they rarely succeed in understanding the logic of public taste. In theory, academic researchers can dig far deeper than practitioners in the commercial world, but they rarely have the resources to do so. There is at present no regular source of funding available for research into the basic structure of higher education in the United States.

Interpreting the Computer Experience at Brown

The Office of Program Analysis of the Institute of Research in Information Scholarship (IRIS) at Brown University was established with the charge of determining the effects of intensive computerization on campus life. We have at present a number of ongoing and completed projects which investigate the academic work patterns of students, faculty, departmental units, academic disciplines, and academic facilities (such as the library). We also survey the campus at regular intervals on computer use and attitudes toward computing to monitor changes from year to year.

The Ever-changing Campus

The overall feeling about computing at Brown is positive. Use is increasing regularly for individuals, but the high level of use and positive feeling may be due to a number of varied causes:

1. Much computing at Brown is a free good for faculty and students. No actual cash is paid by individuals for computer use. Even paper is "free." The faculty is probably paying for this indirectly in lower salary increases over the years, but computing does not have a perceived cost.

2. Computing is a free good for the sciences, too. Computer time can be obtained free or at low cost. However, when serious problems occur, such as system clogging, scientists will complain that the time and effort spent meeting goals is unproductive.

3. Humanities and social science researchers do not generally get new equipment as a matter of course. Grants in these disciplines almost never support purchase of equipment— not even typewriters. Thus, individuals in these disciplines are initially satisfied with little. When things get serious, such as implementing a full departmental computing plan, the demands of humanists and social sciences can be as exacting as those of the engineers. In Brown's case, the music department has been vocal about the difficulties it faced in getting exactly what it wanted for teaching and research.

4. Word processing and spreadsheets are still novel, and few people have hit the peak of productivity with them yet.

5. Lack of good teaching software does not generate complaints. Use of such materials is still considered experimental, and even risky for most instructors, who get no academic credit for their involvement with computing.

Despite these generalizations, we are aware that we are dealing with a moving target at Brown. Student and faculty demands for better computing are growing rapidly, and the mix of computing operations on campus is also changing.

Students are becoming more sophisticated in their use of computing every year. The number of freshmen students reporting computer use prior to entering the university has increased dramatically in the past six years (see figure 1). Now almost 100 percent of students claim prior computer use. Moreover, more than half of Brown's

%

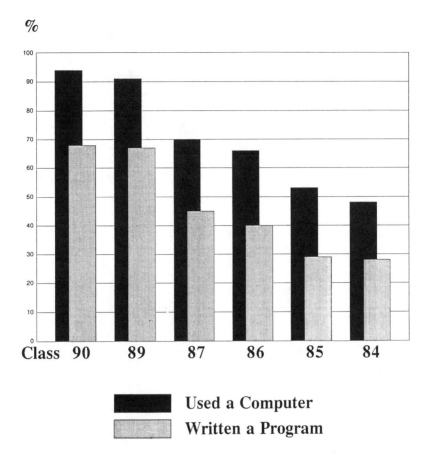

Class 90   89   87   86   85   84

■ Used a Computer
▒ Written a Program

Fig. 1. Freshman Computer Usage Prior to Entering Brown

students are learning their computing skills as early as junior high school. Although women lag slightly behind men, they quickly catch up. The students know what they want, or they already have it (see figure 2).

Overall use is growing on campus, but it is growing more rapidly among faculty and staff than among students. In fact, the percentage of intensive computer users is greater among faculty and staff than among undergraduate students (see figure 3). This is partially because many faculty and administrative tasks can be done using the computer, but there are only a limited number of student academic tasks that the computer can aid. Furthermore, students typically have a limited amount of time to devote to tasks outside of those specifically assigned for course work.

In the not too distant past, Brown was a mainframe-dominated campus for computing operations. The mainframe use has been eroded in recent years by personal computer use, but the three main

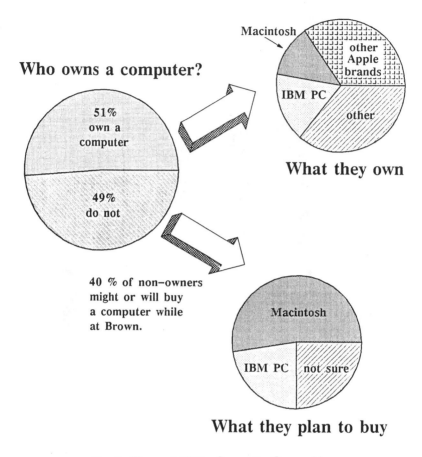

Fig. 2. Class of 1989—Computer Ownership

user groups—students, faculty, and staff—use different combinations of computers (see figure 4). The students are using predominantly Macintosh computers for word processing. The faculty has a mix of Macintosh, mainframe, IBM computers, and others. They use computing for word processing and analysis, and vector processing on the mainframe has increased rapidly despite the decrease in absolute numbers of people using it. The staff use a mix of mainframe, IBM computers, Macintosh, and other computers. They primarily use office functions on the computer: word processing, spreadsheets, database use and communications. The staff is also the primary user of electronic mail.

    Each department and discipline is also different in terms of work habits, depending on facilities and resources. A number of factors affect computer use. The presence or absence of cheap labor in the form of teaching and research assistants is one important factor. These students are often used to maintain and support equipment, and to train other students. Departmental budgets are another factor. Some departments are so poor that they do not have money to purchase tables for computers, much less computer equipment. Finally, the degree of collaboration among colleagues both within and without the university makes a tremendous difference in the quality of computing since the primary source of information about computer use in academia appears to be other colleagues.

Different disciplines publish and disseminate research in different forms. Books are the principal medium for some disciplines,

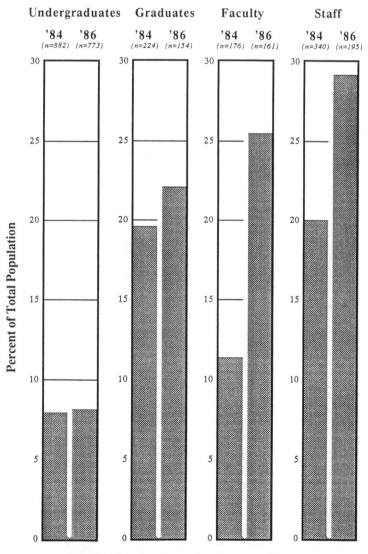

Fig. 3. Intensive Computer Users on Campus
(14 Hours or More Per Week)

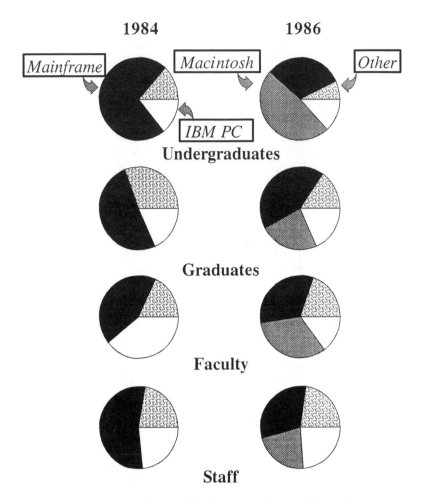

Fig. 4. Machine Use Preference at Brown University

especially in the humanities and social sciences. Short papers are common in mathematics and the physical sciences. Long papers seem to be the principal medium in philosophy and economics, and collective products are common in biology and medicine. All of these forms of publication imply different computing styles. Research styles differ as well. Pure mathematics, for example, does not involve the extensive use of computers in research, primarily because of the nature of research itself. Paradoxically, some of the most exciting computer use is taking place in the arts, where technology has become a new medium for artistic expression.

Pedagogical goals that instructors may attempt to enhance using computers are also very different in different disciplines. Among the range of pedagogical goals we encountered in our research at Brown are the following (there are, of course, many others):

- Increasing creativity
- Achieving competence in base material of disciplines
- Increasing sophistication at problem solving
- Getting students to think like professionals
- Training for a set of specific skills, such as musical skills, for which clear standards of performance exist
- Developing critical thinking skills

Although we know that the campus is a diverse community, we tend to forget this fact when providing tools for that community. We also forget this diversity when we try to assess the change which takes place when new tools are introduced, or to understand why things do not work or are not popular. The academy is not uniform, and experiences will be different for everyone. We need to know enough about campus diversity to understand how to interpret this experience.

Three Projects Studying Campus Life

Studying a Discipline: Art History Program

The Getty Art History Information Program, in conjunction with the Office of Program Analysis at IRIS, undertook a study from January – November 1986 on the work patterns of art historians to prepare for the development of computer-based research tools for art history. Data for the study were collected in two separate operations. The first tracked two research projects in art history based at Brown University for six months. Brown faculty and their graduate students who were involved in the project were interviewed several times over the six-month period concerning the progress and shape of the research. The graduate students kept time and task records of their activities, as well as those of the project supervisors.

The second operation consisted of extensive interviews with eighteen art historians in the United States and Europe concerning their work patterns when conducting research. The interviews, which in most cases lasted two days, yielded over 5,000 pages of transcript material which was analyzed thematically in preparation for writing the final report. The resulting book, *Object, Image and Inquiry: The Art Historian at Work*, has been published by the Getty Art History Information Program (1987).

Art history is a difficult discipline to understand well. Work methods are highly idiosyncratic, and the basic problems of the field are continually undergoing redefinition since they are conditioned by the situation of specific objects in a particular place and time. Problems are also highly contextualized; their solution involves sorting through an infinite number of factors to come to a solution. The scholar's mind is the primary filter for this process. The rest of the process is just "bookkeeping," in one scholar's parlance: sorting references, making footnotes and annotations, and putting ideas into communicable form. Even so, the thought process continues throughout. It does not end when the scholarly product begins to be produced. Scholars in our study of art history report that they often don't know what they know until they have actually written it down.

The primacy of the art object for art historical study is a key to understanding the discipline. For this reason, for many art historians advanced graphic images of art objects have no real use, since no image can ever substitute for the actual art object. On the other hand, computer applications designed to facilitate sorting and organization of bibliographic material and facilitate communication would likely be welcome.

Studying the Effectiveness of a Facility: The Faculty Workstations Project

The geology, chemistry, and music departments recently received IBM RT PC workstations for faculty and student use. We began study of work processes in these departments six months in advance of the receipt of these new computers, and followed the introduction and subsequent use of these new machines throughout the past year. We have recently completed a report documenting the experience of the three departments.

The machine's successful integration into the target departments was dependent on the organizational and work processes in the department, and the machine's fit with those processes. In a department where users knew clearly from the outset what the computers would be used for and where faculty members were used to collaborating with each other to a great extent, the introduction of the workstations was relatively successful. In a department where uses for the computers were clearly known but cooperation and collaboration were not established work patterns, the introduction failed.

Although productivity was increased in the department with the most successful introduction of the machines, the principal effect was the reorganization of work in the departments. The roles of faculty vis-à-vis staff and graduate students were altered considerably as a result of the computer introduction, and important changes occurred in departmental communication patterns.

It is interesting to note that even in the one department where introduction failed, the stimulus of the machines resulted in more productive use of computers, but of a kind different from the IBM RT.

Studying a Computer Research Project: Intermedia System

The most extensive project undertaken by the Office of Program Analysis to date is the three-year study of the development and introduction of the Intermedia system, fully detailed in our report, *Intermedia: A Case Study of Innovation in Higher Education* (Beeman et al. 1987).

The Intermedia project ostensibly involved the design, development, and implementation of a new kind of educational software at Brown. But the experiment was really much more than a new venture in computer-based education. It was also an institutional experiment, an organizational experiment, and ultimately, as well, an experiment in epistemology.

The development of Intermedia took place in the context of a strong history of research in the computing field, but primarily out of two important recent developments. The first of these was advances in the development of experimental hypertext applications for teaching and academic research. The second was the growth of a vision of "scholar's workstation," a computer mounted with an integrated set of tools which could be easily used by academic scholars for a variety of functions.

Intermedia is a set of hypertext applications integrated into a single operating environment, designed to be used by instructors and researchers without need of support from programmers. The system allows the creation of a variety of documents, using the different applications, which can be interrelated through electronic links in many ways. For this implementation of Intermedia, the applications and the types of documents they produce are:

1. InterVal	timelines
2. InterDraw	graphics and diagrams
3. InterPix	digitized images and pictures
4. InterText	written text
5. InterSpect	3-D images capable of 360° rotation

In addition, two utilities were created which enable file management and linking of documents. These are:

1. Folder system	produces graphic images of files and allows browsing
2. Web database map	provides a map of all linkages and a shared database of all links in the system

Intermedia is an open-ended system. Other applications and utilities can be added to it without the need to redesign the entire system. The system is also networked, allowing multiple users to share the same corpus of documents.

The Intermedia system was pilot-tested in two Brown University classrooms in the spring semester of academic year 1986 – 87. The two courses chosen were English 32, "Survey of English Literature II," taught by Professor George Landow, and Biology and Medicine [Biomed] 106, "Plant Cell Biology," taught by Professor Peter Heywood. A third course in music theory was originally scheduled for testing, but could not be accommodated within the development schedule. The courses were chosen because of their size, the reputations of the instructors for excellent teaching, and because they would be taught regularly throughout the development schedule for Intermedia. The two instructors and a number of graduate and undergraduate teaching assistants were compensated during the course of the project for time spent developing course materials.

To assess the implications of Intermedia use, the two courses were studied using both ethographic (intensive participant-observation, intensive interviewing, time-and-task diaries) and survey research methods—a year before Intermedia was used in the classroom, and again during the semester in which it was used. The comparison of the courses serves as the basis for this assessment.

Beyond helping students to read and understand the primary written and lecture materials of their courses, both instructors had specific pedagogical goals they wished to achieve using Intermedia. They wanted students to be able to:

- Synthesize and combine course material in a variety of intellectual contexts;
- Formulate multiple explanations for problems and interpretations encountered in the course;
- Demonstrate an integrated understanding of all of the materials of the course;
- Formulate new and original "critical thinking" about course materials;
- Exhibit this knowledge in professional-level class discussion, paper writing and responses on examinations.

In the report which resulted from this research we characterized these shared pedagogical goals under a term of convenience: *pluralistic learning*.

Intermedia was used by the two instructors in different ways. The corpus of materials developed by Professor Landow for English

32 had a large number of documents of varying quality and density of information, many illustrations and a number of schematic diagrams (or "concept maps") showing the interrelation of topics and materials. The materials for English 32 covered many topics not discussed in the classroom, but related to the critical interpretation of the literature covered in the course.

For Biomed 106, Professor Heywood developed a smaller number of more densely written materials that adhered more closely to the topics covered in the classroom and in course texts. He also included outlines of his lectures and provided links to supplementary materials from them. In neither class was use of Intermedia a strict course requirement, but Professor Landow developed one assignment which required its use, and Professor Heywood devised several classroom exercises designed to be executed using the Intermedia materials. These assignments were not graded.

From student surveys, interviews, and examination of time and task data we discovered that students prioritize their course work rather rigidly. They devote a disproportionately large part of their time to one or two courses, and distribute their efforts in diverse ways among the other courses they may take. For each course they also prioritize the importance they assign to various activities. For English 32, students felt the course readings were the most important aspect of the course; for Biomed 106, they felt that class lectures were the most important.

Students used Intermedia on the average one to two hours per week, and Intermedia use was approximately fifth in priority for course activities in both courses. Student enthusiasm was somewhat dulled because system response time was slow, and because they were uncertain about how Intermedia use affected their course performance (and course grade). Nevertheless, regular student use continued throughout the semester, peaking just before major examinations or deadlines for written class work.

Both instructors were enthusiastic about the use of Intermedia. They felt that it helped them meet their pedagogical goals admirably. Professor Landow felt that student performance in his course was superior to any other time he had taught it. He noticed the difference primarily in student contributions to class discussions but also on written work. Comparison of student response in discussion with English 32 in previous years showed a dramatically increased average number of student comments and questions during discussion in the course taught with Intermedia (see figure 5). The midterm examination in English 32, when taught using Intermedia, was judged to be extraordinarily difficult by Professor Landow's outside grader, who did not know the students. Nevertheless, she was compelled to assign grades higher than the theoretical maximum grade for five students in the course because of the high quality of their performance. The highest scoring students on the examination were among the heaviest users of Intermedia.

Professor Heywood noted that lecturing was far easier because students were using the Intermedia system to prepare for his lectures in advance. He also noted that the professional research papers he requires for the course were greatly improved as a result of student use of Intermedia. In the past, these papers were often turned in long after the end of the semester because students would wait to begin their papers until the topic they wished to study had been covered in class—sometimes not until after midsemester. Using Intermedia, students were able to begin research far earlier in the semester. The end result for Professor Heywood was that term papers, with one exception, were all handed in on time and were of higher quality than in previous years.

Students generally acknowledged the overall value of using Intermedia, but were not always able to specify the exact ways in which it was helpful. English 32 students particularly appreciated the value of Intermedia in providing additional materials. Biomed 106 students appreciated Intermedia's value in reinforcing their

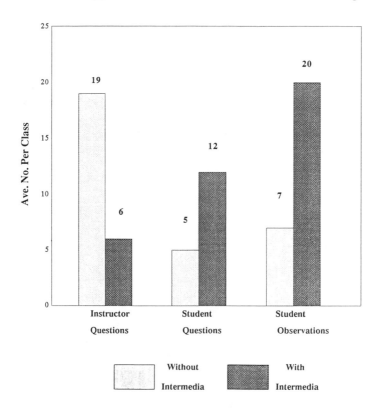

Fig. 5. Effect of Intermedia Use on English 32 Class Discussion

understanding and comprehension of the course subject matter. Students greatly appreciated meaningful documents, and would have liked to have seen more of them in the system. By contrast, they were less enthusiastic about following what proved to be "meaningless links," especially because opening documents was so time-consuming because the system was slow. In neither course, however, did students exploit the system fully; few used every facility available to them. Some of the greatest personal benefits from use of Intermedia were reported by the instructors and teaching assistants who prepared course materials, suggesting that learning might be further enhanced if students were encouraged to use the system to create new material themselves.

Given the limited evidence of two courses each taught only one time, it is not possible to say conclusively that use of Intermedia elsewhere would have the same effects it did in English 32 and Biomed 106. The current version of Intermedia is thus an exciting prototype—but a prototype nonetheless. IRIS hopes to distribute Intermedia to other campuses soon. Much more experience with use of the system in a wider variety of classes, with different instructors, and at different educational institutions, will be needed to further evaluate the highly promising early indications of Intermedia's value for teaching and learning.

Final Lessons

Our research studies have shown us some important lessons for evaluating and assessing the use of computers in academic life. The first is that the campus is an extraordinarily diverse social system, and computers are likely to be used in very different ways throughout the campus. As a consequence, there is probably no universal machine, or universal set of applications, that will work for everyone. For some, the machines will be used like screwdrivers—as tools. For others, such as artists and musicians, they will be used as creative media. For still others, computers with innovative applications, such as Intermedia, will be used as real creative devices to help them think. Campus users will be looking increasingly to applications that are less like tools and more like creative devices and machines to think with.

There is no doubt that computers are here to stay on the campus, but we must be serious about self-study if we are to benefit efficiently and fully from their potential to aid in scholarly work without emptying our institutional coffers. Technology must be in accord with people's real scholarly needs if it is to be efficiently used, and for this to happen we must know a lot more about the academic environment in which computing takes place.

The Changing Library Automation Picture

Richard W. Boss

Local library systems are being used today differently from the way they were used as recently as three years ago. We have moved away from an emphasis on circulation to multifunction, integrated systems capable of supporting acquisitions, serials control, circulation, and patron access catalog modules. Three years ago over 85 percent of all installed systems had only circulation fully implemented. Of the systems installed in the past three years, more than 50 percent have a patron access catalog operational. When circulation is also implemented and integrated with the patron access catalog, the system not only provides access to library holdings, but also to availability information. Most patrons measure their success by how many "available" titles they identify, rather than by the number of entries in a library's catalog.

In the future—as acquisitions and serials control also are widely implemented—patrons will have a window on all of the files of a library through the patron access catalog: on order, in process, at

Richard W. Boss is Senior Management Consultant, Information Systems Consultants, Inc., Washington D. C.

bindery, in circulation, etc. This will make a local library system first and foremost a tool for patrons.

The changing role of automated library systems is particularly significant for smaller libraries. Cost-effective automation of circulation is usually not achieved by libraries with circulation of fewer than 250,000 items a year, and cost-effective automation of acquisitions and serials control is rarely achieved by libraries which purchase less than $500,000 worth of books and journals a year. However, significant benefits can be realized by almost all libraries when an integrated, multifunction system is installed:

- **More access points to holdings.** Catalogs arranged in the traditional sequence—whether in the form of cards or microform—provide only a limited number of access points to the catalog record. A book by Martin Ross with the title *Data Transfer in Analog and Digital Telecommunications Systems* could be found in a card catalog only under the last name of the author, the first word in the title, and the subject headings "Communications" and "Data Transmission." A search under "analog," "digital," "telecommunications," or "systems" would not retrieve anything. In a machine-readable database mounted on a system with keyword searching capabilities, it would be possible to search for and identify the book using all of the access points in the card catalog plus the four additional keywords in the title—all of them terms in common usage today, but not used as subject headings in library card and microform catalogs.

- **More relevant search results.** In a system with Boolean search capabilities it would be possible to execute specific searches, thus reducing the number of irrelevant records retrieved. The following example illustrates the precision of Boolean searching:

	data transfer
OR	data transmission
AND	digital OR analog
NOT	data storage
ONLY	monographs
ONLY	English language
ONLY	published 1978 OR later

  The impact of such capabilities on staff and users can be gauged readily by checking a few items in a card or microform catalog. A mine of information is hidden in the middle of titles and subject entries. Having direct access to this data would enable a library to make better and more extensive use of the materials in the collections and to meet users' needs more efficiently and promptly.

- **Remote access.** An automated system can be accessed from within or without a library.

- **Availability information.** An automated system that includes both patron access catalog and circulation control can provide not only holdings information, but also availability information. The system shows what is out on loan and when it is due to be returned.

- **Greater exploitation of materials through improved inventory control.** The automation of circulation control procedures provides enhanced inventory control through rapid follow-up of overdues, sophisticated fine-tracking capabilities, and ready identification and blocking of delinquent patrons. Automated systems offer streamlined reserves (holds) procedures, enabling library users to obtain materials of interest to them more rapidly. Such systems also can be used to undertake electronic shelf inventories of library holdings, a task often neglected in libraries with manual systems because it is labor intensive.

- **Improved collection development.** An automated circulation control system also has the capability to readily output detailed usage statistics. This capability provides a library with reliable data on which to base future acquisitions and weeding decisions.

- **Improved staff utilization.** Labor savings can be expected as staff are freed from repetitive tasks such as statistics compilation, filing, and the look-up and typing of overdue notices. This function not only requires considerable staff time, but the process is almost always behind schedule. Such resources can be deployed more effectively in more direct service to users. An automated library system with acquisitions and fund accounting capabilities can be expected to improve the management of the library materials budget while decreasing the burden on the staff of repetitive clerical tasks such as filing and typing. Illustrative of the capabilities provided by the automation of acquisitions is the ability to generate claim notices automatically for items on order that have not been received within a library-specified period. Theoretically, such claims could be issued under a manual system, though in practice, few libraries have sufficient staff resources to undertake such claiming. Serials control capability provides a library with the same kind of automated order writing, claiming, and receiving support as for monographs, but augmented with routing and binding support.

- **Funds control.** The sophisticated fund accounting capabilities of such systems provide for the maintenance of more detailed expenditure allocation and tracking records than is normally possible with manual systems.

- **Vendor performance measurement.** Automated systems make it possible to conduct detailed analyses of vendor performance, not only in terms of the speed of delivery of material, but also in relation to the size of discounts provided.

- **Reduction in the rate of staff increase.** A library that automates can expect to enjoy a reduction in the rate at which its staffing requirements increase. The same capabilities that result in the reduction of labor-intensive tasks also contribute to greater productivity in the performance of tasks that continue to require human intervention. For instance, it still will be necessary to staff circulation activities. Automation, however, will result in a reduction of manual procedures so that a single staff member will be able to handle a larger number of transactions than before. Thus, growth in transactions processed can be accommodated without requiring an increase in staffing.

- **Access to other libraries.** The installation of an automated library system not only improves access to the resources of the library being automated, it also offers that library the opportunity to access the automated systems of other libraries using the terminals on its system.

Currently available linkages among automated library systems allow an operator on the terminal of one system to access the database of another system, search that file to see whether that library holds a wanted item, check the availability of the item, and leave an electronic message requesting the supply of the material on interlibrary loan. Training, however, is required to be able to perform these steps. The development of linkages suitable for novices is not yet completed.

The transition from staff to patron tool increases the importance of full bibliographic records, authority control (control of the name and subject headings by which titles can be accessed), full integration of all modules, and user interfaces. While patrons may not want to display full bibliographic records, keyword searching and qualification by year, language, format, etc., will require far more data elements than circulation applications. Quality control will be even more important than in the past, with good authority control, including the ability to make global changes in headings with a single machine action. It will be essential that patrons be able to determine whether a particular issue of a journal has been checked in—periodic transfer of summary information from the serials control module won't do. The extremes of expert and novice modes will have to be augmented with intermediate modes.

The transition to the local library system as a patron tool may increase the importance of personal computers (PC) as workstations. We have been using PCs for several years at circulation to collect charges and discharges when the host system is down. The potential is even greater for patrons. Were some of the so-called dumb terminals replaced with PC-based workstations, patrons could download search results and manipulate them with a text-editing or word-processing package, thus incorporating bibliographic information into manuscripts. Given a gateway through the central processing unit (CPU), they could access remote databases. Searching aids could be provided on the PC. Hopefully, we will move to postprocessing capability: the use of search results from one search to formulate another search. For example, the results of a remote bibliographic database seach could be downloaded and run against the local database to determine which of the citations were available in the local collection.

As patrons become accustomed to using the local library system within the library, they will probably begin to demand remote access from home and office. In most cases that will mean adding dial-in ports to the library system. In some cases it will mean interfacing the local library system with a campuswide local area network (LAN). While most automated library systems have that capability, it is important that terminals in the library not access the library system through the LAN. Instead, a gateway in the library central processing unit should provide terminals on the library system access to the network because most automated library systems are designed to give priority to dedicated terminals—those that have assigned ports on the computer. Those coming into remote dial-in ports or LAN ports only compete for the ports, not for all of the computer's resources.

Patrons may also press for access to the systems of other libraries to look for materials not found in the local database. While librarians may be able to use the terminal-to-computer interfaces now available, patrons will need computer-to-computer interfaces which are transparent—that is, there is no need for the terminal user to know the commands and other unique requirements of the other system. Ad hoc or custom-developed computer-to-computer interfaces should be avoided. Instead, the emphasis should be on conformity to the Open System Interconnection (OSI) Reference Model. The OSI standards—the lower levels of which may be used in all computer applications, and the higher levels of which are specific to applications such as bibliographic record transfer, interlibrary loan— permit heterogeneous or incompatible computer systems to link with one another without requiring special skills on the part of terminal operators. The standards will be usable over LANs within a few miles, over the metropolitan area networks which local telephone companies are now beginning to support, or over nationwide value-added networks (VANs).

As patrons become more sophisticated in their use of local library systems, they may begin to demand more than bibliographic information about monographs. There is no technological reason why journal citation files cannot be made available on local library systems. The major requirements are the development of loader programs, minor modification in the patron access catalog software, and more economical storage devices. Several local library system vendors have already developed loader programs (usually at a cost of no more than $2,000 per file source) and improved searching software. To date, all require the use of magnetic storage media, but there is a reasonable prospect that optical digital disc storage devices will become available from local library system vendors in the next few years. That might make it possible to load large files such as MEDLINE or ERIC on a single optical digital disc, with access from all patron access catalog terminals. This may be more cost *and* service effective than supporting journal citation databases locally on CD-ROM drives attached to PCs.

In the longer term, image databases might also be controlled through the local library system. An image database might be images of pages of backfiles of journals on optical digital disk, or images of slides, photographs or other nonprint materials.

It is unrealistic for a library or a campus to pursue these developments on its own. The key to minimizing the cost and risk is contracting with a vendor which has the human and financial resources, and the interest, to pursue the implications of the transition of the local library system from staff tool to patron tool. While vendors tend to be cautious about making commitments beyond the four major modules (acquisitions, serials control, circulation, and patron access catalog), as more libraries express their interest in future development beyond the core modules, responsiveness is increasing. Several vendors are now signing contracts calling for OSI conformity and journal citation support on magnetic media; some are also pursuing research in optical digital disc technology.

Vendor viability should be a concern when purchasing an automated library system. Of the more than thirty vendors actively marketing library applications software and turnkey systems—those which include all hardware, software, installation, training, and ongoing support from a single vendor—only one in five meets even the most minimal viability criteria. While opinions differ, there appears to be a consensus among library automation consultants that to be viable, a vendor should have at least twenty installations, be selling systems at the rate of at least ten per year, have revenues of at least $3 million a year, be profitable, have completed coding of the four major modules, and have a staff of at least eight committed to software development and maintenance.

While it was common for automated library systems to use proprietary hardware, operating systems, and programming languages in past years to obtain good price/performance, that is no longer necessary. Most vendors now use off-the-shelf hardware and standard operating systems and programming languages. This offers further protection should the vendor cease to be viable.

Library automation is expensive. College libraries seldom recover the full cost of automating their operations because most of them don't have large enough transaction volumes. A decision to automate usually has to be based on the service benefits. A good rule-of-thumb in establishing a budget is $10,000 per terminal for a system configured with sufficient memory, ports, and disk storage to support a 30 percent increase in activity, number of terminals, and database size. A 30 percent increase in activity and database size is usually achieved within two years. The conversion of records to machine-readable form adds another $1.20 per title. Preparation of the computer site costs at least $10,000.

After installation and system startup, hardware and software maintenance is at least $1,200 per terminal per year. While most automated library systems don't require full-time operators, a half-time system manager and two hours a day of operator time should be budgeted.

Solutions that are claimed to cost substantially less than the rule-of-thumb quoted should be carefully examined for incompleteness in functionality, lack of expandability, or lack of vendor support. Particularly suspect are claims that existing hardware can support the library application, thus requiring only the purchase of a software package. That is rarely the case.

Planning for Library Automation

College administrators should consider setting the following planning criteria for library automation on their campuses:

1. The library automation plan should emphasize the patron perspective because improved service, rather than greater staff efficiency, is the major effect of automating a college library.

2. The plan should look at least five years ahead, both in terms of local needs and library automation trends, because that is the timeframe for which reliable data is available and the period over which it is possible to contract for vendor support.

3. The system should be able to support PC-based workstations to facilitate file transfer and manipulation of data at the desktop.

4. The system should be configured to have at least 30 percent spare capacity, and should be expandable beyond that to avoid premature upgrading and/or costly replacement of equipment.

5. The library system should be able to function as a node in the emerging campus network, and in larger area networks for the exchange of information.

6. The system should conform to the OSI Reference Model standards to avoid the development of costly custom interfaces.

7. The vendor should meet minimum viability criteria set by the library to minimize risk.

It is not necessary for the planning of library automation to be tied to other automation planning on the campus if each planning effort has similar criteria established for it. The OSI Reference Model is particularly important in automation planning because it ensures interconnectivity between systems with different hardware and software. Most campuses are too complex to tie everything into a single neat bundle, but it is possible to link components together. Since such linkages can be achieved even over voice-grade telephone lines, decisions about automation should not be held up pending implementation of a local area network.

It is also not necessary to reorganize a library in anticipation of automation. Such reorganization should occur gradually when all library staff have become accustomed to sharing common files. At such time it will be possible to make changes without worrying about the costly duplication of manual files. It will also be possible to provide patron assistance in remote areas of a building with computer terminals instead of with library staff.

While a few institutions have merged libraries and computer centers, or have changed their campus organizational structures so that the two units report to a common administrator, the Association of College and Research Libraries Task Force on Libraries and Computer Centers concluded that reorganization was not necessary if cooperation between the agencies were fostered. Despite the increased use of computers as tools by libraries, they continue to be unique in their functions: the acquisition, organization, and delivery of recorded information. The computer merely makes it possible for a library to perform its traditional role better. The administrators and staffs of 1,500 libraries appear to have successfully automated without changing the relationship to other agencies in the same institution. That is not to say that no changes should be considered, but that a change in the position of a library in a college is not a prerequisite to automation.

Proaction, Liberal Education, and Technology: Institutional and Management Issues for the Undergraduate Institution

Richard A. Detweiler

Much has been written about the impact of technology on education, with most of the focus on the high-tech research universities. Articles are commonly written about the Carnegie Mellons of the world, because of their impressive initiatives with sophisticated workstations, fiber optic networks, and high-level central computing operations. The assumption is that these initiatives represent a true revolution for higher education and describe the future of education generally.

However, this assumption is questionable for two reasons. First, the history of technology-based revolutions in education is certainly unimpressive. Thomas Edison believed that the phonograph would revolutionize education because it would take the voice of the teacher everywhere; within the past twenty-five years video technology was expected to do the same. The phonograph and its technological descendents have certainly caused a revolution, but not in higher education. Video has had an impact on education, but with the exception of a few schools (e.g., the Open University in England), its impact has been supportive or secondary rather than primary or revolutionary. Indeed, it could be argued that the low-tech overhead projector, which took perhaps fifty years to get from the bowl-

Richard A. Detweiler is Associate Vice President for Planning and Communication and Professor of Psychology, Drew University.

ing alley to the university, has had a more general impact on colleges than either of these other technologies.

Second, this assumption is questionable because universities with a high degree of technological sophistication represent perhaps a few score of the more than 3,000 institutions of higher education in the United States. Their focus tends to be on the development and installation of technology in a university context; the vast majority of colleges and universities do not have the orientation, interest, expertise, or resources to undertake these activities.

Is Harvard's Derek Bok correct, then, in his assessment that computer-related technology is being overplayed in higher education?[1] My belief is that he is as mistaken as those who have focused on the technologically leading universities as representing educational role models. The issue is not "what is the impact of technology on higher education" but "what is the impact of computer-enhanced access to information on education." More specifically, what is the impact of enhanced access to information on liberal education?

The fundamental goal of liberal education is to teach people to think. An educated and thinking person systematically, logically, and creatively assesses available information. The current era has been described as the "information age"; it is certainly true that the rate at which information has been added to the base of knowledge has been accelerating exponentially. The result has been increasing specialization and disciplinary narrowness as we have all struggled to keep abreast of our own areas of expertise.

This has posed a particular challenge for liberal education, which by definition tries to educate people widely. We emphasize the importance of broad review, analysis, and integration of information. Yet, unless one believes that the finite world of classical writing in fact defines the universe of knowledge, the sheer volume of information has overwhelmed our traditional methods. Indeed, we now have a revolutionary opportunity in liberal education— the opportunity to use technology to increase the access to and use of knowledge and thereby counteract the narrowness forced on us in recent years by the abundance of information.

My point here is twofold. First, the possibility for educational revolution through computer-related technology is far more substantial for schools of liberal learning than for the technically oriented schools. Second, the nature of this revolution has to do with effective access to broad areas of knowledge, and the ability to communicate efficiently about them. Computer technology is a tool for liberal education.

This tool is not the personal computer or the library automation system or software or the academic computing center; rather it is the integrated use of all of these components. The issues have very little to do with the relatively simple "should we choose a PCclone or a MacIntosh" and much more with "how do we create systems which will take us, in an orderly fashion, from where we are now to some new position when it isn't even clear where we will end up."

I am confident that every college and university will ultimately have pervasive and integrated information systems in support of learning. Some schools have already taken substantial steps; others will do it later. Doing it now certainly has risks, but doing it later has more risks: unless we begin now to build structures, establish educational goals which will guide decisions, preempt idiosyncratic choices of hardware and software by individuals and departments, and, most important, start the process of social change, we will face enormously difficult and complex tasks later on when we will have to begin imposing order on what will have become chaos.

From Solid Systems to Slurry Systems: A Time of Transition

There has been a typical process of change in the management of technology at most colleges and universities. In some cases, these changes have been evolutionary or accidental. In others, they have been part of some longer-range computing plan. The typical undergraduate college began perhaps fifteen or twenty years ago with a single centralized computing center which supported both academic and administrative computing. That was a simpler era when things were reassuringly solid: typewriters were typewriters; programmers were programmers; mimeo was mimeo; telephones were telephones; and mail was mail. About ten years ago most schools began to experience competing demands for system support caused by more sophisticated administrative and academic application software. Programmers were no longer programmers— some were faculty and students with "legitimate" educational goals; others were "merely" staff with rather unseemly businesslike goals. Since it was difficult to support both types of use on a single system, most schools split their computing centers into separate administrative and academic computing operations. At that point, the educational technology world was perhaps the most solid; there existed academic hardware, software, and support, and there existed administrative hardware, software, and support.

In recent years more changes have occurred that have begun to break down these comfortably solid distinctions: typing has become word processing; mimeo has become copying and laser printing; some kinds of mail have become "direct mail" (that is, computer generated); and personal computers everywhere have threatened the control exercised through central academic or administrative computing centers. To further complicate matters, a third computing center is being born on many college campuses as card catalogs and other paper systems are being replaced with library automation systems. Finally, all solid distinctions begin to crumble as campus mail is being replaced with electronic mail through the use of campuswide networks; and Plain Old Telephones (referred to as POTS by nostalgic old phone company employees) are being replaced by "handsets" which no longer pass voices over wires but instead transmit a computerized (digital 1's and 0's) representation of voices.

What was solid is now slurry with the old distinctions blurred: a telephone, word processor, and copy machine are now all computers; both administrators and academics have the same personal computers with the same user training and support needs. Everyone is using the same networking devices. Library automation systems neatly bridge the academic and administrative: they are clearly there for academic reasons but must be run as a production (administrative-like) operation, and they clearly carry out administrative functions with circulation control and acquisitions support.

This, then, is a time of transition. Old distinctions between administrative and academic are breaking down. At the same time, developments in technology and applications combined with the unpredictable outcomes associated with new technology make it impossible to know now exactly what structure makes the most sense.

From There to There

Every college is at some point along a continuum of change, moving from the old *there* of solid systems to a new *there* of slurry systems. The issue is not whether we will end up at a new there since we inevitably will, but rather how we will get from the old to the new. Because we cannot now accurately predict how changes will evolve or what the new system will be like, our challenge is to design a system now which will manage the transition in a flexible, orderly, and effective way.

For each school, designing this system should begin not with an assessment of the existing structure but with a thoughtful decision as to the purpose of technology services for the entire school—a superordinate goal. This must be an explicitly collaborative goal which goes beyond parochial interests. A likely goal for most colleges will be a superordinate academic mission with a somewhat subordinate business goal. It might read something like "to provide the technical resources and support that will optimize the educational process." From this goal, a logical system can be built that will support this mission.

In a small college or university a good system is likely to be characterized by three attributes. First, it will avoid redundancy of support functions and will therefore cut across traditional boundaries (e.g., administrative versus academic or central computing versus personal computing). To have more than one repair center for personal computers or more than one personal computer software support center, for example, is likely to be inefficient and expensive. Second, it will be a flat organizational structure. While it may seem logical to put a hierarchy in place which preserves the current hierarchy within the administrative and academic lines and places a superordinate structure over all, this will be unnecessarily expensive, excessively rigid, and will perpetuate traditional line distinctions. Third, the system will institute fairly general and user-behavior-oriented job descriptions for each employee. Thus, the computer aid station employees' role will not be to "answer questions about the VAX" but to "help solve the problems people encounter in using computing resources."

An organizational concept currently being touted by some major corporations is the "independent operating unit." It seeks to counteract excessive bureaucratization and lack of creativity by creating small mini-companies within a corporation that have substantial independence in product conceptualization, development, and marketing. The strategy being advocated in this paper adopts the de-hierarchical goal but goes in the opposite direction on independence by emphasizing the integration of operations: the "integrated operating unit." Relevant support systems are grouped based on user support function regardless of nominal reporting structure so that systematic planning and support can be maximized and redundancy minimized. As with matrix management designs, a given employee can have responsibilities in more than one unit, and as demands increase or decrease or priorities change, personnel time can be reassigned accordingly. The responsibility of management, then, is to maintain integrated support, allocate personnel time to unit areas, and shift support as needs change.

As technology evolves, it becomes easy to incorporate new needs into this management design. The key factor underlying all these attributes remains the superordinate goal. Having a staff that believes in this goal and is charged with managing a smooth and integrative transition into a technologically integrated future is the key to building a positive and flexible system.

People Come First

Explicit in the previous section is the idea that one must focus on goals to be reached and services to be provided, rather than on traditional line responsibilities or types of hardware or software. This orientation is based on an underlying assumption: the key to the successful integration of technology into an educational environment lies not with technology but with people. This is not to say that the technology is irrelevant—certainly technology which is irrelevant, unreliable, or unsupportable will not help us reach our goals. However, people must trust the technology decisions that are made. In a college, this trust will be established on the basis of different factors for faculty, staff, students, or trustees. But in general, until the reasons for the integration of technology are accepted through the use of an appropriate consensus-building process, attitudes that facilitate productive growth will not emerge.

More importantly, the key to success is to look at all technological endeavors as human endeavors. Avoid being unduly excited by technology itself, but do become excited by what technology can do for education and for the preparation of educated people. Pay more attention to preparing people for the use of the technology through preparatory information, accessible training, and ready support. Certainly, some hardware or software is easier to learn to use than its alternatives, but based on current options, this is a very minor concern. The important factors are not ease of use or quality of graphics display; rather, they are how educated people think and approach information. The effective use of technology requires training if its potential is to be realized.

Finally, we must recognize that this, too, is a time of transition, and what is needed or desirable now may be irrelevant in the future. All members of the collegiate community need to be engaged in the process of discovery.

The Case of Drew: From There to Here

Drew University has traveled a substantial distance from the old *there* of technology. It is deeply into the transitional era, and is in the process of selecting and implementing the last major pieces of the technology puzzle.

Drew is a small liberal arts university with about 1,500 undergraduates and 600 graduate and theological students. It has been described as "militantly liberal arts," and has exhibited the usual unwillingness to support any undergraduate degree program which smacks of professionalism. Indeed, the decision to allow a major in computer science within the mathematics department was made relatively recently and only after a great deal of faculty agony.

The apparent anomaly, then, is that in 1983, the college faculty voted (with only one dissenting vote) to implement the "Computer Initiative." The CI, as it is called, provides every entering freshman with a computer package: a fully configured PC system, printer, and software (WordPerfect, plus Enable with spreadsheet, database, telecommunications, etc.). The full package, including hardware and software, becomes the personal property of the student. The tools are his or hers to use at all times. Students take the PCs home with them during the summers and to jobs or graduate school upon graduation from Drew. This is not an add-on or a required purchase—we have built the cost of this program into our budget and fund it for all students in the same sense that we support the library or other facilities. All of this has been done without any external funding. We have accomplished our goals through tuition set-asides within the normal collegial budgeting process, with a boost from skillful vendor negotiations. We are currently installing a campuswide network for all students, faculty, and staff, and will be following that with a library automation system. How did we get from there to here?

In fact, our story is typical for most liberal arts institutions. What differentiates us is that we made the decision early to take control of computing technology. As of 1970 we had one central computer (an IBM 1130) which supported both administrative and academic computing. It initially had a faculty-director with staff assistance, and later a staff director. An Academic Computing Advisory Committee, made up of faculty, came into being. In the mid-1970s the decision was made to split into two centers, each with its own computer and staff. Line reporting structure was split with the academic center reporting to the college Dean, and the administrative to the Executive Vice-President. The academic center was virtually monopolized by a relative handful of mathematicians, scientists, and social scientists.

In 1981, the university created a University Research operation. It consisted of two psychology faculty members with release time who were charged with carrying out research related to identifying and evaluating the place of Drew University in the educational world. They began providing everyone with ongoing analyses which stimulated a number of creative initiatives. By mid-1983 they became convinced that, given the general trends in technology and higher education, personal computers as a pervasive educational tool made sense. Further, given Drew's place in the educational world, it made sense for Drew to act preemptively. Their advocacy was compelling, and the decision to implement the CI was made by faculty committees, the faculty as a whole, the administration, and the Trustees (with student support along the way) during fall 1983.

The Executive Vice President, a faculty Director, and several other faculty members assumed primary responsibility for program design and implementation, and met frequently to discuss related issues. A large Computer Initiative Coordinating Committee was created which included faculty from across the curriculum, staff, and students. This group met periodically to keep everyone updated and to act on task force recommendations. The major work was carried out by task forces which were set up whenever a problem with no clear solution was identified. Each task force had a very specific and narrow charge, dissolved as soon as it had made a recommendation, and was composed primarily of those most affected by the issue to which it was dedicated (for example, one on "student desks" had only students, the plant director, and Dean of Students; the one on "faculty training" had only faculty; the one on "student training" had both students and faculty). There were literally dozens of these task forces in existence during the first year of the CI. Our goal at all times was to take actions that would foster the use of the personal computer as an information processing tool, as a normal part of one's everyday life—indeed, as a routine part of one's life style.

In spring 1984, every faculty member and staff office was issued a personal computer system, and in September every entering student also received a system. As of September 1987, we reached 100 percent of capacity, using more than 2,000 personal computer systems, with all college students having their own. We anticipate continuing the program for the foreseeable future. Along the way, the transition from solid to slurry began, and the reporting lines were reorganized with all technology-related operations reporting to a vice president (the former faculty CI Director, now in a position that also encompasses universitywide planning and other responsibilities). Responsibilities were redefined in a manner consistent with that suggested in the previous sections. Under this structure, the university will be implementing its "Knowledge Initiative," which will tie all the pieces together through a network with a library automation system at its heart.

Drew has dealt with scores of substantive issues and amassed extensive experience in the selection of hardware and software, faculty and student training, vendor negotiation, software development, cost analyses, software support, the library, and more. We have a full-time staff of only four (director, software librarian, technical person who does all computer repairs, and a secretary) who deal with all personal computer support as well as other central-computer related responsibilities. We, therefore, staff extensively with students for functions such as aid station, training, and programming.

Drew's Impact Evaluation Research: It's a Chair

Prior to the actual implementation of the Computer Initiative, Drew began to collect baseline attitude and use data from faculty and students. Shortly thereafter, the Department of Higher Education of the State of New Jersey funded a three-year study of the impact of the Computer Initiative. To date, twenty-two studies reported in thousands of pages have been carried out by James W. Mills and his associates at Drew on uses, attitudes, proficiencies, benefits, and challenges. Their recent report summarizes their findings, and in fact the state of technology at Drew, by stating:

> Indeed we have found that the use of the personal computer is overwhelming, that people believe in its value, that its use is routine, and that people are about as excited about P.C.'s as they are about chairs—they are absolutely essential but unworthy of too much attention. We believe that this set of effects underlies a subtle but real revolution because it is the adoption and every-day acceptance of any new technology that generates real and often unforeseen change.[2]

Endnotes

1. Derek Bok, "Looking into Education's High-Tech Future," *Harvard Magazine* (May/June 1985): 29-38.

2. *Research Report on the Impact of Campus-wide Computing at Drew University: Final Report* (Drew University, 1988).

Libraries and the New Information Technology: Implications for the Learning Community

Evan Ira Farber

I want to focus on some implications of the new information technology for college libraries and thus for colleges. I am considering the library not organizationally, but as a component of undergraduate education, as a factor in the teaching/learning process. Now, your college catalogs or other admissions publicity may say, or some of you yourselves may have said in speeches or conversations, that "the library is the heart of our college." That's not really the case, though, is it? What is the heart of your institution *is,* of course, that teaching/learning process—those educational interactions that go on between faculty and students, between teachers and learners, in lecture halls, in seminars, in offices, in laboratories, over coffee cups and sometimes (though, of course, not at Earlham) over mugs of beer. It is *that* process that is the real heart of the college.

The library? Its role? Fundamentally, it is to *enhance* that process. Of course, the library has other functions: to provide recreational reading, to collect and preserve the records of the institution

Evan Ira Farber is College Librarian of Earlham College and former President of the Association of College and Research Libraries.

and perhaps of the church or group that sponsors the institution, to provide a place conducive to study, for students and others, even a place to socialize. There are other roles; from the Development Office's point of view, the library may serve as a monument to a major donor. Roles vary somewhat from institution to institution, but the primary, basic role of the college library is to support and enhance the teaching/learning process. How well it does that is the real measure of its worth—not the number of volumes, the luxuriousness of its furnishings, the size of its staff, or the number of periodicals received. Those are all important, to be sure, but no matter how impressive they are, the *sine qua non* for judging the college library is the role it plays in contributing to the teaching/learning process. That, then, is my perspective; it informs almost everything else I say about college libraries and college librarians.

To understand what the new technology can mean for users, it might be helpful to draw a quick sketch of what one had to do to get information just a few years ago. First, one had to travel to the library, which may have been quite distant—or so it seemed, on a cold, wet night—and then not find a parking space. Of course, one could only go when the building was open. To find materials one had to search, at length and with difficulty, catalogs, indexes, and other printed aids. The materials themselves might be in another building, or more likely, either checked out, missing, or being reshelved. Finally, if the material was there, one had to go through the time-consuming process of filling out slips and waiting for the book to be stamped. If the material was not there, one had to go through the really time-consuming process of finding out which other libraries had it, filling out interlibrary loan forms, and then—if indeed it could be found and borrowed—waiting anywhere from a few days to weeks before the material arrived. Today, library technology can eliminate almost all of these difficulties, and in the near future will also have overcome difficulties in getting material that we never even considered trying to obtain.

What are the implications of these changes? There are many, and I want to mention some of the most important. Let's take them up by the group affected—first, the implications for college administrations, then for the students, faculty, and, finally, librarians.

What about the impact on institutions?

One of the important developments for college libraries in the last fifteen or twenty years has been the reluctance or even inability of many colleges to expand library facilities—or, for that matter, almost any facility. It is of course part of the general retrenchment movement in higher education since 1971 or so.

At Earlham, when we were building our library in 1962, we built it on the assumption that we would put an addition on in fifteen years or so. That was the accepted view. For example, Keyes Metcalf, at that time the country's most eminent and respected library building consultant, wrote in his standard manual, *Planning Academic and Research Library Buildings*, which appeared in 1965, that "Libraries have grown rapidly in the past and can be expected to do so in the future. On the average, collections. . . are doubling every sixteen to eighteen years. . ."[1]

And, of course, new buildings or additions to present ones would be built to accommodate that growth. And they were. But, as you know, the picture changed quickly because of demographics, economics, and energy. Whereas in the five-year period 1967 – 71, 257 new academic libraries were built, in the next five-year period the number declined by more than half, and in the 1977 – 1981 period, only 77 were built.

In addition to those factors, the cost of books and periodicals was increasing dramatically, and at about the same time, librarians began to take notice of a number of studies done in the 1960s showing that a small percentage of any library's collection accounted for a high proportion of its use. (This is called the 80-20 phenomenon. The same phenomenon holds in a number of areas. It was first enunciated, as far as I know, in relation to word count—that is, 20 percent of the words in English account for 80 percent of the use. It also holds in retailing: 20 percent of the merchandise in most shops accounts for 80 percent of the sales. I've wanted to test this 80-20 phenomenon in other ways—for example, do 20 percent of our students occupy 80 percent of counseling time? I wouldn't be surprised.) In any case, librarians had known about this ratio—in a rough way, anyway—but had not really focused on its implications. Now, under the pressure of economics, the issue of limiting growth could not be avoided.

In 1975, the Associated Colleges of the Midwest (ACM) held a conference on Space, Growth, and Performance Problems of Academic Libraries. The proceedings of that conference were published under the title *Farewell to Alexandria*. That title alluded to the Alexandrian model that

> to be good a library *must* be vast and always growing. The
> papers presented here examine that faith. . . demonstrating
> that it rests on nothing more than mistaken intuition.[2]

And just a few months later, the Library Administration Division of the American Library Association held a conference titled "Running Out of Space—What Are the Alternatives?"

All kinds of alternatives were suggested—compact shelving, microforms, external storage facilities—but these were really alternative ways of *coping* with growth, not *limiting* growth. They may have been appropriate for university libraries which needed to meet the needs of graduate and faculty research, but not for college libraries. What college librarians began to realize was that part of *their* problem lay in being victimized by what I've called the "university-library syndrome"[3]: thinking of their libraries as small research libraries rather than as teaching libraries. That distinction between the two is clearer now (though still not so clear as it ought to be to many faculty and administrators, I'm afraid) and most college librarians no longer think in terms of continual growth.

This, of course, is where technology enters. With the new information technology, the *operative word for library materials* is "access" not "acquisition." Of course, libraries will keep adding some materials, but they'll be able to meet a substantial portion of users' needs with information that is accessible in electronic form or reproduced from materials in other locations. Combined with new ways of storing printed information on site—that is, transferring material that is seldom used now to say, videodiscs—any college library that has overcome the "university-library syndrome" should be able to settle into a no-growth state. (Not immediately, of course, but in fifteen or twenty years.)

If you administrators are feeling good about all the funds you won't need to spend on a new library or on an addition, or on acquisitions, don't relax just yet. This new technology will not be inexpensive. It's not just the initial outlay for equipment. The building may require some renovation and rewiring, and maintenance and service contracts are costly. While that's still less than a new building, it's not inconsiderable, and the investment will have to be made. Those institutions that don't make it will be severely handicapped in terms of available resources, both for student use and faculty use. They will also be handicapped in recruiting faculty and attracting prospective students, many of whom will have used sophisticated technology in their high schools and will expect it in their college libraries. (The May 1987 issue of *Online* magazine focused on database searching and the use of CD-ROMs in high schools and even in some elementary schools.) Colleges that have not supported their libraries adequately are information-poor now; if they don't invest in the new technology, they will appear even poorer in contrast with other institutions that do have the technology.

The impact on institutions, then, is this: on the one hand, a tremendous potential for information, along with allowance for limited growth; and on the other hand, a necessary commitment to invest in the technology.

What will be the impact on students?

There may well be new ways of learning. While the new information technology may not have so great an impact on ways of learning as the book had, it will still be significant. For example, we have in the reference area of our library several indexing and abstracting services on CD-ROMs. It's been most interesting to watch students use this new technology. First of all, they enjoy teaching each other—and that's good. But even more intriguing is the way they interact with the technology. Whereas with a printed index they would try a few terms and then move on to something else even if not completely satisfied with the results; with the CD-ROMs they keep trying new terms, new combinations of terms. What they're doing, we think, is either manipulating the structure of the database to meet their perceptions of the subject's parameters, or reshaping and modifying their perceptions, or both. This kind of learning hasn't been explored much. The technology permits a kind of interaction with the material that was not possible with print— and with the rapid developments in computer-assisted instruction and artificial intelligence, the possibilities are unlimited.

Whether or not this eagerness to "play around" with information will diminish as the technology becomes more commonplace— that is, whether there's a sort of Hawthorne effect here—I don't know, but right now it's exciting to observe and to speculate about.

What are the potential problems?

Let's picture a college library fifteen years from now that has made an investment in the new technology. We see students in that library who will have available to them information from printed and electronic sources throughout the world—much of that, perhaps, without even going to the library. There are obvious benefits in this—certainly for serious students—but the situation also presents some real problems. For example, let's take a student *today* who is in, say, a course on American foreign policy and wants to do a term paper on U.S. relations with Cuba since 1962. Let's assume he goes to the Library of Congress to do his research. Where does he begin? How does he sort through the thousands of items in the card catalog under "U.S.—Foreign relations—Cuba," or the tens of thousands of articles and newspaper items in the various indexes? To say nothing of the government documents, both American and Cuban. Now consider this: with the new technology, students in 2002 can have all that—and more—at their disposal. How will they know where to begin, how to sort their way through. How can they decide what are the most important, the most useful sources.

There is a student condition, now well recognized, termed "library anxiety." That condition is simply the result of students' lack of understanding, and therefore inability, to cope with the methods and devices of libraries. Students in libraries don't feel in control. In one study done at a small state university, first-year students who recorded their initial response to using the library wrote down words such as "scary, over-powering, lost, helpless, confused."[4] What's the result in their study habits? They naturally try to avoid the library—use it as little as possible, and then badly. This syndrome applies mainly to beginning students, but unless it's corrected, it may last throughout a student's four years. And that study of "library anxiety" was done in a library of relatively modest size. What happens when anxious students are confronted with many times the number of sources?

Of course, one might respond, in fifteen years those students will not be faced with a formidable card catalog and all its complexities. Instead, they'll have terminals, user-friendly terminals, that will probably even help lead the student through a search. (As a matter of fact, The Ohio State University has a FIPSE grant to devise just such a system.) But what does that mean? That the printer attached to the terminal will spew out the information or data, and students, believing that computers can do no wrong, simply accept whatever comes out? That is a result of what I call the "gee-whiz" factor and what Theodore Roszak, somewhat more academically, calls "technological idolatry." That's from his 1986 book, *The Cult of Information*. He describes it as a situation where the computer "can create the impression that students are in touch with a superior, self-sufficient reality inside the machine, a reality which they have the power to control. They need go no further."[5] The subtitle of his book—"The Folklore of Computers and the True Art of Thinking"—should give you some idea of his thesis.

Is this unquestioning acceptance of electronically supplied information, this confusion of data with knowledge, this identification of a simple accumulation of materials with research, better than an avoidance syndrome? Obviously, neither is desirable, and there has to be another way of dealing with unlimited access to information. I'll get to that in a bit.

What about the impact on faculty?

The advantages for the kind of research that depends on printed or archival material are obvious. Allen Veaner, a former university librarian and now a consultant on library administration, wrote a report a couple of years ago on the next decade in academic librarianship. He spoke about this increased accessibility to information, and commented that it could

> exercise a powerful levelling effect in academe. . . . Specialist faculty, graduate students and teaching assistants, and academic librarians in the elite institutions may no longer constitute a premier, invisible academy of gatekeepers or pioneers at the frontiers of knowledge and research. Possibly electronic information systems can democratize aspects of research.[6]

To put it another way, one reason faculty at smaller institutions don't do as much research is the lack of easily available resources. That reason won't hold any more. Will, then, institutional expectations for faculty research change? If they do, and faculty are expected to do more research, what will be the impact on teaching? Another potential problem: might this easier access to materials create tensions between disciplines—that is, between disciplines that benefit greatly from this technology and those that don't benefit as much—and should funds be spent on this technology for disciplines that are literature-based or on disciplines that are laboratory-based? Interesting questions.

The new technology will have, I think, another, different sort of impact on teaching. On the one hand, it will permit a new kind of freedom for teachers—for access to lecture materials, for reserve materials (if, indeed, reserve materials will even be necessary; after all, students will have electronic access also), for materials students can read or use for papers. But what about the problems *created for* the teacher? Will teachers be able to give students guidance in accessing those materials? Will they have to limit the sources students can use? If they don't, how can they evaluate papers based on materials they not only had not read but didn't even know existed? Term papers may even cease to be a viable assignment because of those problems, and because plagiarism will become so easy—and undetectable. The situation will require a different mindset for classroom teachers. Now, when a teacher designs a course, or makes up a syllabus, or devises an assignment, he or she usually has in mind a particular library that the students will use; at least a teacher has a sense of the sources students can find. But with the new technology, it's wide open.

The potential rewards may be great for the teacher who sincerely wants students to go beyond him- or herself and become intellectually autonomous. On the other hand, because the universe of available information will be so large, a teacher who is *just* as dedicated may—in the name of guidance—want to control his or her student's command of that universe, the way a native guide controls the explorer in a vast wilderness.

These are problems teachers never had to think about before, and because the circumstances will be so different from what they are now, may require an entirely new orientation. As far as I can tell, no one has really addressed these questions.

And what about libraries—and librarians?

Most experts on information technology agree that in the near future the general public will access databases directly, without entering a library. It is already happening—just consider the rapidly growing number of individuals who subscribe directly to services such as Dialog or CompuServe, or one of the several thousand other databases providing information on every possible subject. Can the college library be circumvented in searching for information? Undoubtedly, and in fact it already has. A number of faculty and other researchers consult databases from their offices and laboratories. There's not much question that there will be a similar trend among students who will get information dialing up from their own rooms, using a terminal connected with the library's electronic database, or from external databases, or, even more likely, from a combination of the two. David Kaser, a leading library building consultant, said in a recent interview:

> . . . due to [students'] increasing ability to dial up our catalogs . . . and databases from their PCs at home . . . [I] expect that we will need fewer seats in the library than we do now. . . . I [no] longer advocate 33 percent as many seats as FTE enrollment . . . On the average I am probably down around 23 percent and declining slowly.[7]

Wilf Lancaster, of the University of Illinois library school, is probably cited more frequently than any other authority on the future of libraries. He has noted that while the need to visit libraries will be reduced, the need for skilled information specialists will be in great demand. Users may be able to get information directly, but librarians will be needed to guide users as to which databases or other sources to access, to teach search strategies, and to help interpret information.[8] This will be especially true for college libraries, it seems to me, where students will need help and guidance to make the availability of resources meaningful, and to make the process of finding information an educational one.

I am not worried about whether there will be a continuing role for college librarians. I am worried, however, about where those librarians will come from. We have all heard predictions about the coming shortage of college teachers, and most of us are aware that the Ford Foundation, among others, is trying to do something about that. But who is doing anything about college librarians? No one, as far as I know.

The image of the college librarian in faculty and administrative perceptions has not been an especially enviable one. Years ago, Guy Lyle, who was my mentor at Emory University, wrote a marvelously incisive and perceptive little book, *The President, the Professor, and the College Library*, a book still well worth reading. In it, he quoted Julian Boyd, the distinguished Princeton University librarian and historian, who had spoken of the "view," held by too many presidents, "that . . . librarians are technicians, far below the rank of policy makers. They are to keep the machinery going, to chart its mileage per gallon, to change its tires, and to keep it ready-fueled, but not to touch the steering wheel." And, Lyle added, "this is a view frequently held by faculty members."[9]

That comment was made some twenty years ago, and though attitudes may have changed some, they have not changed enough. I think, though, that you'll soon begin to see a more rapid change. The impetus of the bibliographic instruction movement—its increasing recognition by the various disciplines and its demonstrated success on individual campuses—will begin to make it a part of many college teachers' stock in trade, and so faculty will be working more closely with librarians in educationally creative ways. The new library technology should also contribute to a changed perception of librarians. Not only will librarians be increasingly looked to as guides—for both faculty and students—through masses of information, but in an important way the respective roles of classroom teachers and college librarians will come closer together. That role is teaching students that there is a difference between information and ideas, between data and knowledge, and that one needs not only to be able to find information and to collect data, but to sort it out, relate it, understand it, and use it to help create new ideas, to gain knowledge and understanding.

Librarians enjoy another advantage. As Roszak points out, "By virtue of their training and experience, [librarians know] when *not* to use the computer," but rather when it's better to use monographs and reference books, periodicals, archives, or even to consult experts.[10] And for a long time, librarians will have to live in both worlds—a nineteenth century one, so to speak, of books and periodicals that have not yet and perhaps never will be processed by computers, and the twenty-first century—where all this marvelous technology will do much of their work.

The library as we know it today will not disappear—not for a long time, if ever. It is, after all, not just a place for machines to store and retrieve information. It is also a human institution. Paul Lacey, who teaches English at Earlham, gave a talk a few years ago entitled "Views of a Luddite."

> I am not conceiving of the library as an information retrieval system primarily but as a social system. . . in which retrieval of information is only a part of the goal. Browsing, conversation, exchange of ideas, sharing and confirming values, supporting one another in the common enterprise of study, reflection, and publishing one's findings—these are extremely important to what a humanist, or any member of the scholarly community, does. . . . I am arguing that the library is not merely a place or a collection of functions but a living symbol of valuable and rich human relations. . . . In our work as teachers and as researchers we know something of the joy of self-transcendence, being caught up in a text or a search that makes us forget ourselves, and we also know the joy of com-

munion, of finding kindred spirits, dedicated scholars and writers who are a part of our human family. There must be places where such things can happen and be confirmed and memorialized. Universities and colleges are such places. So are libraries.[11]

Technology *will* have a profound impact on what college libraries can do and how they do it. Users will look for and get information very differently, but the library as we know it today—for a long time to come, at least—will still be a place to study, to browse, to think, to relax. "A library," Robert Frost once said, "should be the place where the student has it out with himself."[12] For a college library, certainly, that role, permitting a student "to have it out with himself," is much too precious to lose.

Endnotes

1. Keyes D. Metcalf, *Planning Academic and Research Library Buildings* (New York: McGraw-Hill Book Company, 1965), 9.

2. Daniel Gore, ed., *Farewell to Alexandria: Solutions to Space, Growth, and Performance Problems of Libraries: ACM Conference on Space, Growth, & Performance Problems of Academic Libraries, Chicago, 1975* (Westport, Conn.: Greenwood Press, 1976), [3].

3. Evan Ira Farber, "College Libraries and the University-Library Syndrome," in Evan Ira Farber and Ruth Walling, eds., *The Academic Library: Essays in Honor of Guy R. Lyle* (Metuchen, N.J.: Scarecrow Press, 1974), 12–23.

4. Constance A. Mellon, "Library Anxiety: A Grounded Theory and Its Development," *College & Research Libraries* 47 (March 1986):162

5. Theodore Roszak, *The Cult of Information: The Folklore of Computers and the True Art of Thinking* (New York: Pantheon Books, 1986), 70.

6. Allen B. Veaner, "1985 to 1995: The Next Decade in Academic Librarianship, Part I," *College & Research Libraries* 46 (May 1985):225

7. Administrators' Update: "An Interview with David Kaser," *Library Administration & Management* 1(3) (June 1987):77.

8. F. Wilfrid Lancaster, "The Future of the Library in the Age of Telecommunications," in Donald W. King, ed., *Telecommunications and Libraries: A Primer for Librarians and Information Managers* (White Plains, N.Y.: Knowledge Industry Publications, Inc., 1981), 150–1.

9. Guy R. Lyle, *The President, the Professor, and the College Library* (New York: The H. W. Wilson Co., 1963), 22.

10. Roszak, 174.

11. Paul A. Lacey, "Views of a Luddite," *College & Research Libraries* 43(2) (March 1982):118.

12. Address at the dedication of the Gordon Keith Chalmers Library, Kenyon College, Oct. 28, 1962. I don't know if the text of the address exists, but I made a note of his comment when I heard it.

Liberal Education and Information Technology: Today and Tomorrow

James W. Johnson

Ten years ago, French President Valéry Giscard d'Estaing commissioned Simon Nora and Alain Minc to write a report on the impact of information technology on French society. The resulting book, *L'Informatization de la Société,* described the marriage of computer and telecommunications technology as a force comparable to that of electric power in restructuring French society. The report was serialized by a Paris newspaper and helped set a national policy that greatly increased use of computing and communications technology in what is perhaps the most technophobic of Western nations. The results in France have been significant.

Like France, America's colleges and universities face the need to understand and harness information technology to maintain their role and place in the world order. Our colleges and universities, particularly liberal arts colleges, face a technology that appears to be alien to their traditions and values of humanity and civility. For France and for American colleges, finally, electronic technology is an expensive venture for frugal economies.

James W. Johnson is Vice President for Computing, University of Houston.

Information Technology and Liberal Education

That computing and related information technology has been reluctantly accepted, if not resisted, by liberal arts colleges is understandable. Early college use of electronic technology in the 1960s suggested that it was of little importance to liberal learning. Most widely used in applied fields such as business administration, engineering, and computer science, where computing was an object of study, it had few early applications in core areas such as mathematics, history, literature, and physics. In support of teaching, it provided drill and practice for rote tasks in a mechanistic fashion—an approach alien to the liberal arts tradition of stimulating thought through close student-teacher interaction. Electronic learning options such as the use of television to teach large numbers of students in a simple session with a mission of liberal education were not likely to capture the imagination of faculty at colleges.

Despite these widespread misgivings about information technology, several college faculty began to make exciting use of technology in support of undergraduate education. Dartmouth College, for example, was an early leader in computer augmented education, as were Grinnell College and Reed College. (One of my first experiences with computers was at a Grinnell College symposium in 1968 celebrating the opening of its computing center. A featured speaker was from the Mannes School of Music.)

Yet even at these schools, a tension existed between what was happening in the classroom and traditional college values. In 1970, I headed a computer-based education program at a small college. More than 50 percent of all undergraduates used the computer in one or more of their courses. Students were using computers for creative projects such as an analysis of Richard Nixon's speeches or an econometric model of the U.S. economy. In the same year, however, the college won an award for an advertisement showing a punched computer card torn in two and saying, "at our college you are more than a punched card." The irony is clear and tension between using computers and preserving a system that values individual attention to students is obvious.

Today, there is growing recognition that information technology cuts to the core of higher education. As Nobel Laureate Herbert A. Simon of Carnegie Mellon University has stated, "Nobody really needs convincing these days that the computer is an innovation of more than ordinary magnitude, a one-in-several centuries innovation and not a one-in-a century innovation or one of these instant revolutions that are announced every day in the papers or on television. It is really an event of major magnitude." Use of the computer, the keystone of modern information technology, is no longer restricted to applied disciplines, rote learning, and mass education.

Kenneth Wilson of Cornell has suggested that there is a new science emerging, computation science, that will take its place alongside mathematics as a new method of representation offering scientists new tools and insights. Combined with graphics, computational science offers a new way of looking at the world; already scientists using this technology report a qualitative improvement in their research.

Computing, together with electronic communication and electronic information storage, may be a liberating experience in the same way that reading a book or travelling is liberating: it provides students access to a world that extends beyond their direct experience and can be viewed through a different perspective. Imagine students having at their desks immense computational power; the ability to communicate their ideas to other students, perhaps across the continent; access to the world's libraries; and/or ways to observe three-dimensional color pictures to enhance their intuition. If information technology provides such a broadening, eye-opening opportunity, it has a profound role to play in liberal education at any institution.

Troubling Thoughts

Perhaps because information technology is a force of major magnitude, it raises perplexing questions, both philosophical and pragmatic. Some of these concerns include the following:

- The technology is constantly changing. New waves of superior hardware and software appear almost daily. Will a college's investment of scarce resources become instantly obsolete? Should colleges wait until the pace of change slows down and the field becomes more stable?

- Educational gains for the new technology are not clear. How has the use of technology improved the education we offer our students?

- Overall computing expenses at colleges are increasing despite decreasing per-unit costs. An automated library seems to cost more than the old one. Computing costs have increased 11 percent per year over each of the past two years. Faculty request $5,000 to $10,000 "workstations" where $2,000 "personal computers" used to suffice. How much is enough?

- Organizational boundaries between academic and administrative computing, libraries, computing centers, data communications and telephone systems are blurring. Furthermore, new disciplines such as computational science or biophysics, with a common thread of numeric methods, are emerging. How should colleges be organized to accommodate these changes? How do we attract and keep people with new, scarce, highly sought skills to manage these environments?

- How can colleges maintain a balance between historic enduring values and a tradition of giving students time to reflect, and the rapidly changing, fast-track, current-time orientation of technology?

This article and those that accompany it will provide insights for answering these questions. They will *not* answer them. The issues involved are complex and the institutional and disciplinary settings diverse. Each college will have to adopt its own strategy. But just as no two colleges are identical, no college is entirely unique—all gain from sharing experience and examining the work of leaders in the information technology arena. The task here is to provide a broad overview of information technology in higher education. Given the breadth of information technology, this is a humbling assignment. The difficulties of predicting the exact course of technological development are obvious. Yet if the focus is on concepts underlying the technology and on long-term trends rather than short-term changes, progress becomes comprehensible.

Information Technology's Four Facets

The so-called new information technology consists of four key elements: computing, communications, information storage, and information science. Together, they form an integrated technology more powerful than the sum of its parts.

Computing

The key to the new information technology is the computer. Computers provide intelligence by being able to carry out "if this, do that" types of operations. By following simple instructions at rapid speed, computers can select, amplify, and transform information in digital form. In a crude sense, computers allow people to manipulate information in the way that steam engines allowed us to manipulate physical objects. (The analogy is crude because moving information is extremely rapid and it is nondestructive.) The impact of computing is amplified when the base of information is in digital, or machine-readable form; it is increased when information can be moved from place to place via electronic communication, and it is increased when it is transformed into rules of information science.

Communications

The ability to move information from place to place has the effect of increasing society's information base and rendering distance an obsolete factor. Quantitative increases in communications speed and capacity make qualitative differences. Consider the difference between a Morse code description of an event in Paris and a satellite-transmitted television broadcast. Like information storage, communications is increasingly occurring in digital form with the advantage that it can be stored in a common format for retrieval by computers.

Information Storage

The ability to record and store information so that it can be moved from place to place, from time to time, and from one person to many people has been a major development in human society. Writing, the printing press, the photograph and the moving picture have been major contributions to the maintenance of society's record of ideas, accomplishments, and events. The current trend is to store all types of information—text, pictures, and voice—in digital form in small packages. The results make more information available, more cheaply, in a form that can be rapidly selected and analyzed by computers.

Information Science

Information science is an ill-defined field that embraces concepts and disciplines that make significant contributions to the use of computers and communications power to perform useful tasks. Included are areas such as cognitive psychology, philosophy, linguistics, developmental psychology, and neurophysiology—all providing insights as to how we think and how we can utilize tools to help us think. Also included are more applied fields such as information engineering, computer science, decision theory, and data structures. While the field may be ill-defined, the multidisciplinary efforts of thousands of researchers seeking to improve human intellectual productivity are a driving force behind effective use of new technology.

Costs and Convergence

The French have a word, *télématique*, that they use to describe information technology. It is commonly translated as "computerization" and as such loses its real meaning. It really signifies the four facets of information technology, not simply computers, working together. And it is this integration that makes the technology such a potent force. The digitization of information and the almost universal use of digital computers to process it have blurred the distinctions between telephone, television, radio, and print technologies.

Not only do the elements of information technology build on each other, but they also fall in per-unit costs at the rate of about 25 percent per year, or eighteen times per decade. Thus, the power of a $2,000 computer is increasing dramatically, and the cost of storing a page of text electronically is falling just as dramatically. Communications costs are also declining annually. Not only are these trends likely to continue over the next decade, but breakthroughs in photonics (the use of light) may accelerate performance/cost particularly in information storage and communications. Largely because of these declining costs, use of information technology will continue to increase. As a result, total expenditures for technology will continue to increase.

Currently, information science is the "bottleneck" information technology. Productivity gains are modest and far outstripped by demands for increasingly complex software, ironically, to achieve user simplicity. But improvements are coming in the form of computer aids for software design, durable and detailed technical standards, reusable software components, and standardized interfaces.

Current Status, Trends, and Policy Guidelines for Colleges

While information technology must be taken together, for purposes of analysis, computing, communications, information storage, and information science will be treated separately.

Computing

Current Status

The dramatic increase in computer use in American colleges over the past five years has paralleled the rise of personal computers. While in 1980 fewer than 3 percent of American professors had their own computers, today more than 60 percent do. More than 20 percent of students have their own personal computers. The machine of choice has, until recently, been the IBM PC, but as more software has become available, the Apple Macintosh is now becoming the system of choice among faculty and students because of its superior display, better printing, and ease of use. At the research level, the preferred unit is the Sun Microsystems Workstation, offering the power of a minicomputer such as a Digital Equipment VAX on the desktop. The Digital Equipment VAX is the dominant shared computer, achieving mainframe status at small campuses. IBM mainframe computers are most popular at large universities, but represent a declining share of the total computing market. The market position of computers is important because it determines where the most software will be available.

While computers are heavily used for word processing, they are also used by faculty for class notes, display statistics, and database access. Among social scientists and humanists, about 65 percent report that computers have improved their research and 20 percent report that they have improved their teaching. These numbers are probably greater among scientists and professionals.

Although 20 percent of college students have their own computers, colleges and universities provide an average of about one computer station per twenty students. At large universities, the average may be as high as forty students per station, and at small colleges the average is closer to ten students per station. A few colleges and universities have a strategy of one student/one computer. A more common goal is three or four students per machine.

Computer literacy for all students is no longer an issue at most colleges, since virtually all entering students have had computer "literacy" courses in high school as well as a course in "keyboarding skills" (a fancy label for touch-typing). What is important is computer use in specific academic disciplines and courses. Here the largest use is in business, engineering, and computer science, where students learn programming and package use to solve problems. But computing is equally important in statistics and increasingly important in writing. In the sciences, the use of computers for analysis and simulation has long had a foothold.

Computer-assisted instruction, using the computer as a learning aid, has yet to emerge from its infancy. It has been most successful in military training and remedial education. In these instances the learner is "controlled" by the machine. A more promising approach might be having students use the computer as a tool to navigate through information or to explore simulated worlds. The work being done at Brown University, reported in this volume, is a good example of this new approach to computers and learning.

Trends

A new wave of small computers called "workstations" is now reaching the marketplace. They offer minicomputer power, high-quality sound, high-resolution graphic displays, high-resolution laser printers and built-in hardware and software to connect to networks. Their power and storage capacity will be used for easy-to-use software, graphics, and multimedia access. While it will be three to five years before a full range of software is developed for this new wave of computers, the new software will be qualitatively better than old software, and will overcome many current obstacles to truly effective computer use.

With the development of workstations and high-speed communications will come highly specialized machines to hook onto the network as "servers." A good example is the so-called mini-supercomputers offering extremely high-speed computations for a class of problems previously unworkable on all but the most powerful supercomputers. Other examples include database machines, exotic printers, and gateways to worldwide data networks.

The next wave of computer technology promises to provide undergraduate students with tools previously available to but a handful of researchers. Combined with communication technology, this wave may bring a world of information to the desktop.

Policies

In a workstation-network environment, the entire network becomes the "computer," and the network should be the focus of the computer center. In addition to building, operating and maintaining the network, computer center staff must work in concert with resource suppliers to set standards for hooking up administrative databases and library catalogs and databases to the network.

In addition to setting standards, college computing policies should recognize that:

1. Software is the name of the game. Systems should be selected that provide a base of existing software and the promise of new software. In addition, the budget must take into account expenses for software, just as it does for hardware.

2. The technological life of most computers is five years, and the economic life about seven years. Plans must allow for yearly turnover of equipment. Further, where the current "standard" equipment is installed, a modest investment should also be made in state-of-the-art equipment to allow faculty and students to become familiar with it.

3. A compatible family of computers that allows connection and focusing of human support is an important strategy. Using an array of computers that can't be connected, each with a different set of programs and operating systems, is a sure way to dilute scarce resources. The trend here is toward Macintosh-like displays, the UNIX operating system, and TCP/IP (Transmission Control Protocol/Internet Protocol) communications protocol.

4. Computer gifts in the form of used equipment are often Trojan horses hiding high operating and maintenance costs.

After seven years replacement of old equipment usually pays for itself in the savings in operating and maintenance costs.

5. Hardware and software must be matched by "peopleware." As a rule of thumb, two to three support people to answer general questions and keep equipment operating are required per 100 *additional* workstations.

Communications

Current Status

Communications technology in the form of telephones, radio, and television is a mature technology. But recent changes in communication media and the addition of computer technology are radically altering traditional communications services. As a field, communications technology is today where computing was in 1970—but it will be the key information technology of the 1990s.

In a sense, communication technology today is in an embryonic state. Educational television as a mass medium has remained stable since the 1960s. About 20 percent of faculty and student computers connect to computer networks. Most of these networks provide low-speed terminal access to computers. Electronic mail is used by fewer than 10 percent of the university community. Electronic networks are commonly used for interlibrary loans—a widely used method of increasing the resources available to local faculty and students. Two national networks, BITNET and ARPANET, provide low-speed connection of about 2,000 colleges and universities worldwide.

Many colleges and universities are in the process of wiring their campuses for high-speed communications. At the departmental level, many units have installed local area networks for sharing data and printers providing electronic mail. Unfortunately, these networks often suffer from lack of management and seemingly unreliable performance. Among local area networks, the most popular are Apple-Talk and those based on Ethernet. Telephone systems continue to play a key role in providing all types of communications including voice, data, facsimile, and slow motor video.

Recent technological and regulatory changes challenge traditional views of communications. Television is no longer simply a one-way, mass communications technology. The VCR renders television more responsive to individual controls and also makes it an information storage—as well as delivery—medium. The video camera moves production from the professional studio to the individual amateur. High-speed communications via fiber-optics cable makes it possible to move images from one location to another. It is often economically attractive for organizations to build and operate their own communications system, including telephone.

Trends

The digitization of communications will continue with voice, data, and images being transmitted as 0's and 1's for easy computer storage and processing, Digital television is perhaps a decade away because of the tremendous investment in equipment that is needed.

Along with digitization will come increased speed, allowing transmission of pictures rather than characters. As transmission capacity increases, the statement that distance is obsolete will become even more true. One notable example is the National Science Foundation (NSF) networks tieing together regional NSF networks at speeds of more than twenty-five times those of existing networks. The NSF network will transmit about forty pages of text per second.

As networks become faster, easier to use, and cheaper, a growing number of specialized resources will be connected to them. These include databases, supercomputers, and mail systems.

Policies

Colleges must recognize that communications technology is strategic to their future. Faculty often complain that they feel isolated from colleagues with similar scholarly interests and that resources such as book and journal collections and databases are not adequate for research. Connection to regional and national networks will be an important way of reducing isolation of both faculty and students and providing access to a growing body of resources.

Colleges are encouraged to:

1. Develop a long-term communications plan. Such a plan is needed because it takes a long time to implement new systems and they last for decades.

2. Investigate ways of wiring their campuses so that every office and every residence hall room has access to high-speed communications networks. Participation in regional and national networks will be crucial in the 1990s.

3. Recognize that opportunities exist for economic cabling in combination with energy management, security, cable TV or the telephone system. For most institutions, replacing the telephone system offers the best opportunity to cable for the future and save money as well.

4. Engage outside expertise for help in developing a plan in this specialized area. One possibility is the EDUCOM consulting group, a reasonably priced, educationally focused source of help.

5. Use standard protocols that are vendor-independent, such an Ethernet or TCP/IP for the campus network.

Information Storage

Current Status

Information must be in machine-readable form to be processed by computers and transmitted at near the speed of light. In this form it may be selected and searched in ways that are impossible manually. Today a limited amount of society's information is machine-readable, but the base is growing rapidly. Virtually all publications are now produced by computers and thus are machine-readable, and scanning equipment for converting printed text to magnetic storage is becoming more accurate and less costly.

About 1,800 databases containing either bibliographic or actual text information are readily available and used by about one-third of the scholarly community. Libraries are beginning to make these databases available locally—usually stored on compact discs, read only memory (CD-ROM) discs like the compact discs that are replacing records and tapes for audio recordings.

Data available for computer processing is overwhelming in character form. Until recently, images and sounds have required too much space to be stored economically. Most data is stored on magnetic disks that store up to one million characters for a few dollars in easily transportable form. In fact, it it actually less expensive to store data on a magnetic disk than it is to store it on paper, and it takes less space.

Access methods to data stored on computers are still relatively slow and cumbersome, relying on indexes to provide searches in fewer than 10 seconds. Hypermedia is a good start in trying better ways of accessing information by providing relational links rather than linear indexes.

Trends

Machine storage of information is rapidly becoming a superior technology that will displace current technology. High-resolution displays, typeset quality printers, and optical storage devices all team together to overcome earlier disadvantages. Of particular interest is the possibility of storing sounds, pictures, and movie pictures on the same device as text and data.

Existing devices that point the way to the future include CD-ROMs storing 256 million characters of data, and videodisks storing 54,000 frames of television pictures. Access methods are improving and full-text searches in reasonable time periods are within reach. Within the next two years, the power of connecting computers to large amounts of information will become clear as new products reach the marketplace.

The largest barrier to widespread use of machine-based information will not be technological, but legal.

Policies

New information storage technology is likely to have a dramatic and perhaps liberating intellectual impact on education. Surely colleges and universities that have long measured quality by their library resources cannot debate the value of rich information resources. But information storage technology will have organizational impacts as well. Libraries, in particular, will be called upon to both master new technology and function in their traditional role of nurturing an increasingly complex set of holdings including books, journals, software, databases, video recordings and more.

Colleges and universities must stay abreast of developments in information storage technology and encourage its development. They should:

1. Develop formal or informal structures that bring together libraries, computing, and audiovisual service personnel to discuss trends and coordinate plans.

2. Experiment with new technologies such as intelligent video-disk systems, CD-ROM, hypermedia, and expert searching techniques.

3. Expand library holdings to include electronic media.

4. Establish policies that protect intellectual property rights so as to encourage publishers to experiment with new technologies.

Information Science

Information science is a label used to identify a group of emerging disciplines such as computational sciences, computer science, and cognitive science that build on more established fields such as mathematics, linguistics, and psychology. Information science is significant because it seeks to better understand how people think, solve problems, and interact with intellectual tools.

Current Status

Impressive work is taking place on several fronts, notably in ease of use, expert systems, intelligent tutoring and computational science. The results of ease-of-use research are readily apparent in devices such as Apple Computer's window displays using icons. Expert systems are effective in limited domains for solving well-structured problems using simple decision rules and large amounts of data. The best example is XCON, which is used to configure working computer systems from an almost endless combination of components. Intelligent tutoring systems for teaching subjects such as algebra are being tested. Computational science is providing scientists with new insights into complex phenomena such as fluid flow dynamics, molecular modeling, seismic analysis, and weather forecasting.

Trends

This field is so new that there are few trends. Instead there are disappointments where there was promise and unexpected breakthroughs where there were seemingly insurmountable barriers. Two areas of great promise are pattern recognition including voice and data recognition, and natural-language processing. Both of these areas will provide the added benefit of insights on how human beings carry out these complex thought processes almost instantaneously.

One of the most fascinating aspects of this area is the use of information technology to build and test models of human cognition, providing cognitive scientists with a laboratory that was not previously available.

Policies

A reasonable strategy for any institution of higher education faced with demands to offer the latest new discipline, or new disciplines, is to focus on enduring, fundamental subjects and not chase the latest fads. Not only is this reasonable but it is also wise. Students need, above all, to be adaptive. Yet the information sciences are so fundamental to human thought, and underlie so many other disciplines, that thought should be given to making an exception. A college should not attempt to build a cognitive science department. But it should try to stimulate existing faculty and bootstrap development in this area. A sensible course may be to:

1. Have a faculty member begin summer study in this field.

2. Install an artificial intelligence system or related software on campus.

3. Create study groups to explore the new field across several disciplines.

4. Involve students in research projects in information science.

Where Does All This Lead?

This article has emphasized three themes. First, previously separate technologies are converging to create a powerful new technology described by the French as *télématique*. Second, the technology is driven by falling costs, increasing capabilities and new scientific research. Third, the technology is significant because it deals with intellectual activity.

So what, you may ask. Information isn't important anyway, knowledge is. Besides, universities have survived so-called revolutions for over 600 years.

Three lessons suggest that we need to think about this revolution.

Information Is Important

A basic tenet of Western society has been that more information is better than less. Those who challenge this view should be asked this question: if they were suffering from an apparent heart attack, would they rather go to a physician in 1776 or 1988? Most would answer 1988. But why? Are today's physicians any smarter? Not likely. But today's physicians have an advantage. They have the record of what previous generations have done—what has worked and what has failed. If they are lucky, they know the consequences of what their predecessors have tried. Building on the record, as well as challenging and retesting the record, is a major element of our progress as a society.

And progress it is. Despite the faults we often find with highly technological societies, including our own, the fact is that the most advanced societies can also be the most humane. They have increased mutual well-being and reduced misery and poverty. They evince the greatest concern about assaults on the environment and on fellow human beings. They have provided social welfare and medical services for all segments of society. And they have allowed the greatest freedom of thought and the greatest measure of equality.

Transforming Technologies

Students of technology tell us that technology often goes through three stages, although few reach stage three—perhaps only a few each century.

During the first stage, a technology replaces an old way of doing things by doing it better, faster, or cheaper: automating an accounting system or replacing copper wire with fiber optics substitutes superior technology for old technology. Such new technologies are sometimes called "killer" technologies, because they kill the old way of doing things.

In the second stage, technology does new things that were not previously possible. Examples include airline reservation systems, high-speed computation, word processing, and interactive graphics. Each is a killer technology in replacing old methods of paper and pencil or crude mechanical devices, but each offers enhancements that make a qualitative difference—such as page printing, spell checking, and grammar analysis connected to word processing.

Some technologies do new things but do not replace old methods; they are often called "niche" technologies.

The third stage is one of transformation. In this stage the technology transforms our way of life. The truly profound technologies begin as improvements or killer technologies, or as niche technologies, but become transforming technologies. For example, the steam engine was first used to pump water from mines; but its greatest impact was in transforming the rate of transportation from four miles to forty miles an hour. The printing press was first used to improve the accuracy of transcription for the few scholars who could read; it transformed all of Western society. The air conditioner replaced nothing, but it filled a niche; ultimately it helped change the population distribution of the United States if not the world. The automobile replaced the horse, reduced distance, and continues to influence everything from where we live to how we court.

The lesson here is that the most profound results of technology are unpredictable and unintentional. Information technology has already replaced, improved, and transformed, but the most significant results are yet to come.

Thinking About What We Do

Alfred North Whitehead once observed that society makes progress not when it thinks about what it does but when it doesn't have to think about what it does. There is much truth in Whitehead's statement, particularly if lack of such reflection signifies the existence of common purposes and consistent methods. Information technology has always forced institutions to think about what they do and how they do it, however. Higher education should be no different.

In considering the importance of information, being prepared for unintended consequences and thinking about the mission of one's institution, college administrators should reflect on Clark Kerr's words:

> The external view is that the university is radical, the internal reality is that it is conservative; the internal view is that it is a law unto itself, the external reality is that it is subject to forces of history.

In considering information technology as a force of history, colleges and universities are well reminded of computer scientist Joseph Weizenbaum's admonition:

> The great matter of our time lies in the differences between information, knowledge and wisdom; between calculating, reasoning, and thinking; and finally in the difference between a society centered on human beings and one centered on machines.

Maximizing the Potential of Technology

Patricia C. Skarulis

The past ten years have been marked by fundamental changes in information management and movement. Colleges and universities are information-intensive environments, and as such have felt the effect of these changes. The opportunity to provide a new and exciting scholarly environment exists, but the cost of technology is the limiting factor. This paper will provide some practical suggestions for incorporating technology into the campus environment.

Scholar workstations are the fundamental tool for gathering, analyzing, and communicating information. Faculty can review current literature with the aid of compact disc technology and with online access to libraries. Engineers can use computer-aided design tools to model the effects of earthquakes on building design. Radiologists can use supercomputers to generate three-dimensional images and can display those images on high-resolution graphic workstations. Economists and statisticians can evaluate trends and develop models using external databases. Researchers from across the country can coauthor articles using electronic mail facilities.

Patricia C. Skarulis is Vice President for Information Systems, Duke University.

Faculty and students can interact using this same mail facility. Faculty advisors can obtain current information about their student advisees. Principal investigators can determine the current status of their grants. Purchase orders for equipment can originate and flow through the institutional approval process without ever having to be retyped. All of these applications are possible with today's technology, but the faculty/student scholar needs to be able to move from one application to another and from one computer environment to another almost effortlessly. To form a seamless environment, it is important that the institution bring academic and administrative computing together with library automation.

While the new technologies have been embraced by faculty who have found a new way to increase their productivity or have found it possible to pursue new areas of research, the most enthusiastic champions of technology on campus are our incoming students. They are comfortable and familiar with computers. Most have been exposed to computing in the sixth through eight grades, and many even earlier. They are unintimidated by technology; they see it as just one more resource to be understood. Consider for a moment how young people approach machines in video arcades. While an adult may look for instructions giving the rules of a particular game, young people readily put their quarter in the machine and experiment to learn the rules—the same way that they learned to walk when they were toddlers. As a result, these students have an intuitive feel for using technology. It is natural to them.

However, one of the main problems facing colleges and universities today is how to afford the extraordinary costs of technology—costs which did not exist twenty years ago. In the late sixties and early seventies, a campus would face the costs of financing a new computer once every seven years—or so we hoped; that cycle soon decreased to every five years. Now we are seeing three-year cycles. Almost as soon as a computer or lab of computers is acquired, it is out of date.

When calculating the costs of technology, it is important to take into account the hidden costs: staff, software, building renovations, and more. For example, when budgeting for personnel, in addition to counting those persons in the organization with formal computing titles, it is important to include persons with a variety of other job titles who spend a significant amount of time programming or managing a computer for their departments or divisions. Software for microcomputers can be deceptively expensive. If a software package for a microcomputer costs $100, but there are 100 microcomputers on campus, that cost becomes $10,000. There are building costs associated with renovating classroom space and dormitories to accommodate microcomputers—not only to provide the space that they require, but also their electrical needs and the networks to hook them together.

One way of creating a seamless environment and at the same time containing costs is to appoint a single person to oversee information technology issues. Typically, that person would be responsible for all academic and administrative computing, telecommunications, and, in rarer instances, managing the library itself. Even if it is not feasible to pull all of these functional areas together in a single organization, someone should be designated to act as a chief information officer and coordinate all technological activities.

One of the primary duties of the chief information officer is to coordinate the various computing needs on campus and integrate them into a cohesive institutional plan. In developing a plan, some of the major questions that need to be asked are as follows: How many computers are really needed for faculty and students? Of what type? Where should they be placed? Who should have access to them? How should they be funded? Should students be required or encouraged to purchase their own computers? What is the appropriate and economical networking strategy? How do these plans relate to library automation?

In many cases the best answer is not always self-evident. Logical arguments can be given for a number of different approaches. The issues often involve many areas of responsibility, creating another level of complexity in seeking solutions. Added to these considerations is the certainty of technological change that rapidly renders the best answers obsolete. What is needed is a carefully considered, coordinated approach that addresses the issues in a logical sequence: a systematic plan that keeps the institution moving ahead even if it does not attempt to deal with all the issues at once.

A natural outgrowth of the plan should be a set of standards for the institution. By having a plan and by ensuring that computer purchases fit within that plan, the institution can maximize its resources. For example, a campus standard may generally limit the purchase of microcomputers to one or two manufacturers, thus maximizing the discount potential for the school.

One of the ways of saving money and maximizing the value of the dollars that are spent is through careful negotiation with vendors. It is important that a school take every advantage of volume discounts, donations of equipment, and joint research projects. Each of the major computer vendors have special programs for higher education, and in some states private institutions can buy off of the state contract. Some schools have entered partnerships with a single vendor to provide technology at a substantial discount in exchange for using the campus as a demonstration site.

There are, of course, foundations both corporate and private that may be able to support special programs. In general, however, they are besieged with requests. To be successful, a project must fit in with the goals of the foundation and generally be unique— difficult criteria to meet. It may be possible to package existing resources in a new or unique way to generate revenue. For example, local industry might be persuaded to help support library automation in exchange for online access to the college or university library. Some entrepreneurial faculty and staff envision developing the next Lotus 1-2-3 and making a substantial royalty for the college. It is rare that software developed on campus becomes a commercial success, and yet those few institutions that do succeed often make a great deal of money. It can be a full-time job representing the institution to the outside world, and yet it is one that pays for itself.

Most colleges have learned to carefully evaluate the hidden costs in the gift of used equipment. Often the maintenance costs on such equipment are prohibitively high, or a specialized computing environment must be provided for the equipment. Some schools, however, do not carefully consider the hidden costs in gifts of new and desirable equipment. For example, schools that received large grants of microcomputer equipment might not have considered how much staff time would be required to support the equipment or the cost of remodeling classrooms and buying furniture to accommodate the equipment. Once the equipment is two- to three-years old and needs to be replaced, they realize that the capital costs have not been accommodated in the college's budget. Obviously, most institutions would accept the gift of equipment if given the choice, but they need to be realistic in recognizing the hidden costs.

As part of its technological planning, the institution needs to review its telecommunications strategy. The options include installing a Private Branch Exchange (PBX), moving to Centrex with the local operating company, or integrating voice and data through the same telephone switch. Each of these alternatives can be attractive under the right circumstances. Unless the college or university is large or complex enough to have a good degree of in-house expertise in this area, it is probably best to hire an outside consultant. Some schools have reported that the mere rumor that they were putting together a request for proposal (RFP) caused their local operating company to make an aggressive bid for a Centrex system which lowered their rates considerably.

One good source for consulting advice is an institution's alumni/ alumnae, especially those in business. Another source is technology experts in local corporations. Both groups are often able to tap the resources of their companies for help and expertise in specialized areas. It could be extremely helpful to establish a Technology Advisory Board that meets once or twice a year to review plans, suggest directions, and potentially help obtain resources to implement the institution's plans.

In today's environment, excellence in instruction and research requires first-rate tools for processing, retrieving, and communicating information. While sophisticated computing facilities and networks alone do not ensure top echelon standing, their absence will deny an institution an opportunity to improve and compete nationally. The demands of today's information explosion necessitate that colleges and universities have the ability to organize, store and retrieve staggering amounts of data, to subject them to previously impossible computational processes, and to communicate them rapidly and efficiently across the campus and nation. The university that cannot perform these tasks will rapidly find itself unable to fulfill its mission.

Appendix A
Conference Directory

Members of the Advisory Committee

Patrick Barkey (deceased May 17, 1988)
Director, The Honnold Library, The Claremont Colleges
Executive Office Associate
OCLC Online Computer Library Center, Inc.

Deanna B. Marcum
Vice President
Council on Library Resources

James L. Powell
President
Franklin and Marshall College

H. Paul Schrank
Former Vice President, Membership and Corporate Relations
OCLC Online Computer Library Center, Inc.

JoAn S. Segal
Executive Director
Association of College and Research Libraries

Members of the AAC Staff

Shelagh M. Casey, Meeting Coordinator

John W. Chandler, President

Joseph S. Johnston, Jr., Director of Programs

Daphne N. Layton, Assistant Director of Programs

Nora P. Topalian, Administrative Assistant

Institutional Participants

Washington D.C. Conference, June 19–20, 1987

Dickinson College

George Allan, Dean of the College and Acting President

Thomas Burtnett, Director of the Computer Center

Annette LeClair, Chairperson of the Department of Library Resources

Pamela Rosenberg, Coordinator of Academic Computing

Neil Weissman, Professor of History and Coordinator for International Education

Hollins College

Paula P. Brownlee, President

Bridget Puzon, Dean of the College

Richard Kirkwood, Librarian

Robert H. Hansen, Director of Academic Computing Services

Edwina Spodark, Assistant Professor of French

Mary Washington College

William M. Anderson, Jr., President

Philip L. Hall, Vice President for Academic Affairs and Dean

LeRoy S. Strohl, Library Director

William R. Pope, Director-designate of Academic Computing

James E. Goehring, Assistant Professor of Religion

Nazareth College of Rochester

Rose Marie Beston, President

Richard Del Vecchio, Director of Strategic Planning

Richard Matzek, Director of the Lorette Wilmot Library

William Nass, Director of Computer Services

Edith Kort, member of the Mathematics/Computer Science Department and Database Instructor

Paine College

William H. Harris, President

Roger Williams, Dean for Academic Affairs

Milli Parker, Head Librarian

Alice Simpkins, Director of Information and Computer Science Programs

Carol Rychly, Assistant Professor of Mathematics and Director of Institutional Advancement

Randolph-Macon College

Ladell Payne, President

Jerome H. Garris, Dean of the College

Dan T. Bedsole, Library Director

T. Boyd Moore, Computer Center Director

Elsa Falls, Professor of Biology and Chairman, Resources and
Plans Committee

Union College

John S. Morris, President

Thomas D'Andrea, Vice President for Academic Affairs

Jean K. Sheviak, Coordinator of Online Systems and Head of
Technical Processes, Schaffer Library

David Cossey, Director, Computer Center

Shelton Schmidt, Professor of Economics

University of Scranton

Rev. J. A. Panuska, S.J., President

Richard H. Passon, Provost and Academic Vice President

Glenn Pellino, Vice President for Planning

Kenneth Oberembt, Director of Alumni Memorial Library

Jerome DeSanto, Director of Computing Systems

Columbus, Ohio Conference, November 8–9, 1987

Bradley University

Martin G. Abegg, President

Kalman Goldberg, Acting Provost and Vice President for
Academic Affairs

Joel L. Hartman, Associate Provost, Information Technologies
and Resources

J. Michael Yohe, Director, Computing Services

Gerald Dillashaw, Associate Professor of Education and
Associate Dean, College of Education and Health Sciences

The College of Wooster

Henry Copeland, President

Donald W. Harward, Vice President for Academic Affairs

Patricia Rom, Director of Library Services

Carol Zimmerman, Director of Academic Computing Services

Robert Smith, Chair of the Faculty Library Committee

Earlham College

Richard Wood, President

Leonard Clark, Provost and Dean of Academic Affairs

George A. R. Silver, Director of the Computing Center

Evan Ira Farber, College Librarian

Jerome Woolpy, Professor of Biology and Philosophy,
and Coordinator of the Microcomputer Laboratory

Kalamazoo College

David W. Breneman, President

Timothy Light, Provost

Eleanor H. Pinkham, Director of Libraries and Media Services

Richard D. Piccard, Director of Educational Computing

Jan Tobochnik, Assistant Professor of Physics and Computer Science

Kenyon College

Philip H. Jordan, Jr., President

Reed S. Browning, Provost

Harlene Marley, Interim Director of the Libraries

Thomas Moberg, Director of Academic Computing

Russell Batt, Associate Professor of Chemistry

Knox College

John P. McCall, President

John Strassburger, Dean of the College

Douglas Wilson, Professor of English and Director of the Library

William D. Ripperger, Associate Professor of Mathematics and
Computer Science, and Director of the Computer Center

Richard Stout, Assistant Professor of Economics and member
of the Task Force on Academic Computing

Loyola University

James C. Carter, S.J., President (unable to attend at last minute)

George F. Lundy, S.J., Senior Vice President and Dean of Faculties

Mary Lee Sweat, University Librarian

Herbert Nickles, Director, Academic Computing Services

Gary B. Herbert, Associate Professor of Philosophy

Rosary College

Jean Murray, O.P., President

Norman Carroll, Vice President for Academic Affairs and
  Dean of Faculty

Inez Ringland, Director of the Library

Gerard Mikol, Assistant Professor of Chemistry and Coordinator
  of Academic Computer Services

Cyrus Grant, Assistant Professor of Computer Science

Participant at Large:

Hannelore Rader, Librarian, Cleveland State University

Pomona, California Conference, February 22–23, 1988

Grinnell College

George Drake, President

Charles Duke, Dean of the Faculty

Jane Tederman, Director of Computer Services

Gail Bonath, Assistant Librarian for Technical Services

Emily Moore, Assistant Professor of Mathematics and Chair,
  Faculty Academic Computing Committee

Lewis and Clark College

James Gardner, President

Jacquelyn A. Mattfeld, Provost/Executive Vice President

Clarence Davis, Dean, College of Arts and Sciences

Randy Collver, Director of the Watzek Library and Academic Computing

Leslie Baxter, Associate Provost/Director of Planning and
  Analytic Studies; Associate Professor of Communications

Loyola Marymount University

Rev. James N. Loughran, S.J., President

Rev. Albert P. Koppes, O. Carm., Academic Vice President

Richard Perle, Director of Campus Computing Services

G. Edward Evans, University Librarian

Stephen Scarborough, Professor of Mathematics

Mills College

Mary S. Metz, President

Stephen S. Weiner, Provost and Dean of the Faculty

Steven Pandolfo, College Librarian

Carol Lennox, Director of Academic Computing

David Roland-Holst, Assistant Professor of Economics

Mississippi College

Lewis Nobles, President

Charles Martin, Vice President for Academic Affairs

James Burnside, Director of Academic Computing

Rachel Smith, Librarian

Glenn Wiggins, Professor of Computing Science

Occidental College

Richard C. Gilman, President

David Axeen, Dean of Faculty

Jacquelyn Morris, College Librarian

Thomas Slobko, Professor of Mathematics and Director,
  Computer Center

Saul Traiger, Assistant Professor of Philosophy and Director,
  Cognitive Science Program

Reed College

Paul E. Bragdon, President

Victoria Hanawalt, Librarian

Gary Schlickeiser, Director, Academic Computing

Stefan Kapsch, Professor of Political Science

Sonoma State University

David W. Benson, President

Milton Gordon, Vice President for Academic Affairs

Susan Harris, Director of the University Library

Richard Karas, Professor of Physics and Dean of Administrative Services

Appendix B
Institutional Profiles

The profiles in this appendix are grouped by the OCLC/AAC Regional Conference attended.

Conference 1, June 19 – 20, 1987, Washington, D.C.

Dickinson College

Dickinson College is a private, residential college in Carlisle, Pennsylvania. Since its founding in 1773, the college has had as its mission educating undergraduates in the liberal arts. It offers a full range of basic liberal arts programs, with a special emphasis on international education. With a student body numbering approximately 1,900, the college has a faculty of 145, supported by 26 academic professionals. Dickinson uses two central computers, one MicroVAX, 200 microcomputers, and 150 terminals.

Academic computing at Dickinson has been experiencing rapid growth in the number and diversity of microcomputers, microcomputer and central computer software, and users. In the past year, the college has gone from a one-computer (DEC Rainbow) to a three-computer (Rainbow, Macintosh, and IBM-compatible) environment. We attempt to retain word processing compatibility with WordPerfect software for all three environments. Microcomputing primarily encompasses word processing and communications, and, to a lesser degree, spreadsheets, graphics, and databases. Six computer rooms house approximately thirty terminals and sixty microcomputers; about twelve more microcomputers are available in the library for use with the automated catalog. Currently, sixty-four faculty and academic professionals have been assigned microcomputers. The student-per-micro ratio is approximately 30:1, and about 40 percent of the academic staff have college-purchased microcomputers. We offer students and faculty discount purchasing plans for several types of microcomputers, but we do not anticipate requiring students to purchase computers.

The central VAX 8800 is heavily used for electronic mail, word processing, and administrative computing, and also for statistical computing and department-specific software. VAX resources such as number of logons and disk space are limited. We hope to move the student word processing that is still done on the VAX to microcomputers. Even so, VAX usage will continue to increase due to growing use of the automated library catalog, statistical analysis of large datasets, and administrative computing.

Academic computing expenditures have been primarily for systems acquisition, and have not included adequate resources to support sustained growth. We lack routine budgets to provide existing microcomputers with software and peripherals, and sufficient personnel to comfortably support instructional research and program growth. Computer Services currently has two positions providing user support—each shared between academic and administrative computing.

AutoCat, the online library catalog system developed at Dickinson with support from the Pew Memorial Trust and the Digital Equipment Corporation, is currently available in an advanced prototype version through more than 200 microcomputers/terminals around campus. It features keyword searching, full Boolean logic, numerous indexes which can be limited by format, language, and branch library, online help, record editing capabilities (including for foreign languages, the use of all diacritics), and interactive authority control on names, subjects, and subject phrases. The library uses the OCLC Cataloging and Interlibrary Loan Subsystems and completed a retrospective conversion project in 1982. Free database searching services are also provided through DIALOG.

Dickinson has never formally implemented a campuswide data communications network. This means we are still in the advantageous position of having few pre-existing communications protocols that constrain our future plans. Despite the lack of local area networks, we do have a "network." Our VAX 8600, PDP 11/84, and MicroVAX II are in close proximity, allowing a tightly coupled DECnet connection. A user of any system may be given access to the other systems via the network. Files may easily be transferred among these three systems, as well. Thus, we have a single centralized computing utility that provides support dependent upon the application, for example, computer science courses on the MicroVAX, administrative applications on the PDP 11/84, and everything else on the VAX 8600. All our terminals access this computing utility either through a dedicated port or via dial-in lines; about one quarter of our microcomputers are also directly connected. Thus, we have enough of a "network" to allow widespread use of electronic mail, library catalog access, file sharing, uploading, and downloading.

We have been working this year [1987] on a master plan for computing and telecommunications. Its purpose, besides the substance of the recommendations it contains, is to improve the processes of decision making on these matters. Our current processes have been sufficient to assure cautious but constant growth in the quality and quantity of campus computing. But that success and the endless revolution in computing technology have made it clear that we must rethink our procedures as we reexamine our long-range goals.

Dickinson expects to decide soon how best to furnish the campus with voice and data communications systems (or system) that are available in student dormitory rooms, all faculty and staff offices, and relevant classrooms and laboratories. Future plans of the college also include completing programs for the full version of AutoCat, the addition of other modules to create a fully integrated library system, and the introduction of online reference and other services through the campus electronic mail network.

We would like to have sufficient academic user-support personnel to increase basic services such as consulting, computer classes, user documentation and newsletters, and to implement intersession and summer faculty computing workshops. A campuswide computer committee has recommended that we improve the ratio of students to publicly accessible microcomputers from 30:1 to 10:1, and that we increase the percentage of faculty and academic professionals who have college-purchased microcomputers from 40 to 80 percent. We hope to be able to support the routine use of large databases, desktop publishing, and networking. Finally, several departments have expressed interest in powerful computers capable of running artificial intelligence and sophisticated graphics software.

Hollins College

One of the oldest women's colleges in the nation, Hollins College is dedicated to fostering academic excellence and humane values through a liberal education. Hollins offers bachelors degrees in twenty-two fields and limited masters programs to its 1,000 students. Approximately eighty FTE faculty teach at the college.

Hollins has a strong commitment to using computers as a tool for quality education. The college has a DEC VAX 11/780 and three MicroVAXs with associated terminals and peripherals, an IBM-PC laboratory, and small numbers of other microcomputers. The computing facilities are extensively used by departments across the college, including Art, Economics, English, Political Science, Psychology, French, Mathematics, and Computer Science. The writing center and the library are also active users. In addition to the facilities provided by academic computing, many departments have one or more microcomputers for academic use.

Library automation, to the extent that it exists, has been developed independently of the campus computer center, except that computer terminals tied to the college's mainframe facility are available in the library for faculty and student use. Computers are used internally for various administrative functions, such as budgeting and fund accounting. Catalog card production and interlibrary loan are performed online through SOLINET, the OCLC-affiliated regional network, and the OCLC system, and online bibliographic searching through DIALOG. Serious damage to the library from flooding in November 1985 has inhibited the development of plans for further automation of library functions until the library's holdings can be restored.

Hollins College installed a fiber-optic-based Ethernet backbone in the fall of 1986. This network connects all of the terminals, the VAX 11/780, three MicroVAX I machines, and the IBM-PC laboratory. Approximately 25 percent of the full-time faculty have immediate access to the network via a terminal on their desks or in an adjacent laboratory. A major use of the network is the research under way at Hollins in computer-based education. This work is supported by Hollins and uses equipment provided in part by a Special Investment Grant from the Digital Equipment Corporation. This research is providing operational experience with the network and the MicroVAX computers.

Development in the near future will focus on the evaluation and acquisition of software. The college will continue to support the integration of computer/network technology into classroom instruction across the curriculum.

Mary Washington College

Mary Washington College is a state-supported liberal arts and sciences college in Fredericksburg, Virginia. In fall 1986, the college had 146 full-time faculty; 2,774 degree-seeking undergraduates, two-thirds of them living in dormitories; 115 degree-seeking graduate students; and 303 special students. Approximately 25 percent of the residential undergraduates come from outside Virginia. The college offers thirty-five undergraduate major programs in twenty-one departments; its limited graduate offerings are designed for part-time, commuting adults.

Our Administrative Computing Center is based on a high-end Hewlett-Packard minicomputer supporting ninety-two users in nineteen application areas. The Center is currently developing software which will do degree audits and allow academic advisers to match student credits against degree requirements in various programs, seeking the best fit. To be fully useful, the system must be accessible to faculty advisers across the campus.

The Center operates three PRIME minicomputers on a proprietary token-passing ring network with a dozen dial-ups and approximately fifty terminals located around the campus. It also manages more than fifty MS-DOS microcomputers. Its users include faculty, students, and anyone using word processing.

Our library is well on its way to a complete online catalog using the Virginia Tech Library System (VTLS). We are also able to download bibliographic data from other VTLS libraries directly into our database. The system is at present supported by Administrative Computing hardware; the college will purchase a dedicated minicomputer for the library in fiscal year 1988. As soon as most of the library collection is available online, we will want to make the catalog accessible from dormitories and academic buildings.

Coordinating these activities is the Dean's Advisory Committee on Computing Resources, which includes all members of our conference team except the college president, as well as the executive vice president and the assistant dean for programs and projects.

Our immediate plans call for the addition of about fifty microcomputers, some on local area networks and others connected to the larger Prime network, during summer 1987. The directors of Academic and Administrative Computing have also begun planning for the campus network.

Nazareth College of Rochester

Nazareth College of Rochester was founded in 1924 by the Congregation of Sisters of St. Joseph of Rochester for the education of women. In 1969, the governance of the college was turned over to a lay Board of Trustees, and in 1974, men were admitted to Nazareth's full-time undergraduate program so that today it is classified as an independent, coeducational institution that emphasizes career preparation solidly based in the liberal arts. The college has about 1,450 full-time undergraduate students and about 900 part-time graduate education students. The college has a full-time faculty of 108 persons, the majority of whom have been at the college for ten years or less. This latter fact is a reflection of the establishment of new programs in the social sciences and business since the mid-1970s.

In regard to academic computing, the college initiated a formal planning process in 1984, the product of a two-year study by a major faculty task force. The plan defined the requirements for student computer literacy and the general academic computing needs of students and faculty. The computer literacy program consists of a twelve-hour workshop for incoming freshmen to introduce them to our Macintosh, Apple, and mainframe computers, and taking one course of which computer utilization is a component. The college has a dedicated academic computer, a VAX 11/750, with several statistical and database packages and numerous programming languages. It also has four microcomputer labs: a Rainbow laboratory of twenty machines mainly for the business department, a lab of ten Apple IIes used primarily by the education department, ten Macintoshes for general student use, and a library facility with Apple and Macintosh systems for general use. Complying with the task force's recommendations, the college has also created twelve faculty Apple and Macintosh clusters, some of which have access to the mainframe. Approximately fifteen to twenty faculty have microcomputers and/or VAX access directly from their offices. Recently added or approved facilities include a desktop publishing facility, an AppleTalk network for the Macintosh lab, and a small facility of four or five IBM-compatibles.

Ongoing and future academic needs are addressed through two committees. One is a committee of liaison faculty from each department who meet collectively with the Academic Computing Coordinator to discuss specific programmatic needs. The second is a committee of four faculty and the Academic Coordinator who monitor and address computer literacy requirements and more comprehensive institutional academic computing needs.

Since September 1986, the Lorette Wilmot Library has operated an online public access catalog (LS/2000 system, distributed by OCLC) with eight public terminals in the library. Online circulation is now accessible through the LS/2000 system with the exception of serial holdings, which are scheduled to be made available shortly through an OCLC system. For seven years, the library has provided a heavily subsidized online searching service which has benefited, in particular, the large part-time student population in the graduate education program. The library operates two public access microcomputer laboratories and has ordered desktop publishing equipment for student use. Currently under study are remote access to the online catalog and the employment of CD-ROM technology for direct user access to research materials. Lastly, in June 1987, four multifunctional workstations with high-quality print capability were installed by the Xerox Corporation in response to a successful grant proposal.

The present state of networking on the campus is through an arrangement of multiplexors and data switches, which allow individual stations to have access, as permitted, to several systems. Electronic mail has recently been added to our system, but limited access of faculty to computer consoles has inhibited wide use of this service. Our isolated AppleTalk network is limited to the Macintosh lab.

For now, Nazareth seems to have met its needs in academic computing equipment and services. The future challenge is less a matter of acquiring more equipment than of making more effective use of existing resources. In effect, our technical capability is in excess of our capacity to use it. The next agenda for the Academic Computing Committee and the Academic Computing Coordinator will be the examination and implementation of a program for encouraging and training faculty to better utilize our computers.

The college is presently exploring avenues of implementing a Decision Support System (DSS) for strategic planning purposes. This will allow users to have direct access on an ad hoc basis to administrative files on the mainframe. While this is mainly an administrative need, there will be in all likelihood a spillover effect in the academic area since academic departments have similar informational needs. Moreover, much of the software used in DSS, e.g., spreadsheets and data management systems, are relevant for academic computing as well.

In sum, Nazareth has experienced in the last three years an accelerated growth in the purchases of academic computing equipment, the development of the computer science major and a graduate education program in computers in education, major advances in library automation, intense utilization of computers by the Math/ Computer Science and Social Sciences Departments, with more modest investment by the Business Department, and seminal steps toward the implementation of a Decision Support System on campus.

Paine College

Founded in 1882, Paine College is a four-year liberal arts institution affiliated with the Christian Methodist Episcopal Church and the United Methodist Church. It is historically biracial in establishment and leadership and predominantly black in enrollment, which is currently almost 800 students. A full-time faculty of fifty-three guides students through an extensive core curriculum and thirteen majors. While maintaining its deep commitment to the liberal arts, Paine has strengthened its programs in the preprofessional sciences and business administration. Adaptations to the curriculum have included spreading an understanding and appreciation of the value of technology across the liberal arts core.

Academic computing at Paine College is supported by microcomputers, mainly Apple IIe and IBM Personal Computers (or compatibles). These seventy-one computers and peripherals are housed in three microcomputer laboratories and in various faculty offices. Computer activities further two major college goals: the development of campuswide computer literacy and the development of computer-related emphases that are designed to provide graduates with the background to complete a major in information systems or computer science. At present, computer literacy applications range from word processing and database management to computer-aided design. One introductory and eight application minicourses in support of the computer literacy program were recently added to the curriculum.

A grant from the Sloan Foundation provided funds that permit us to decentralize the use of computers in the academic area. Microcomputers are now being placed in classrooms and faculty members are being trained to use the computers' powers of rapid calculation to solve problems during class discussions and demonstrations. Two computer-related emphases, information systems in business administration and computer science in mathematics, have also been added to the curriculum. These emphases permit students to select a computer-related focus in their major field of business administration or mathematics. Our most recent effort to utilize the powers of the computers in academic matters centers on our new Test Skills Development Center in which we will utilize computer programs in our efforts to improve the overall performance of our students on a wide range of standardized tests.

In administrative computing, the networking system at Paine College is controlled by an IBM System 36 with one megabyte of memory and 400 megabytes of storage. Twenty-eight terminals are connected to the mainframe, allowing senior administrators and other program officers representing ten areas to communicate directly with the system.

All terminals are cable-connected and an additional forty-four terminals can be added to the system. The features of the system include interaction with a common database, electronic mail, word processing, and uploading from a PC to the mainframe and downloading from the mainframe to a PC. The online application software includes the Comprehensive Integrated Student Records System (CISRS, pronounced "scissors") registration, payroll, alumni and development record-keeping, financial aid, the general ledger system, student accounts, admissions, grade reporting, transcripts, and other administrative services.

Since 1972 the library has been a member of the Cooperative College Library Center (CCLC). CCLC is a nonprofit organization that performs technical processing (acquisition and cataloging) for forty-two colleges at a cost-effective rate. Eighty percent of the books added to our library since 1972 were acquired through CCLC and are in the OCLC database. Our library also has access to DIALOG, the online bibliographic search service, and we are currently testing an automated circulation system in the college's Learning Resources Center.

In our continuing effort to ensure that our system will effectively serve the needs of our faculty, students, and administrative personnel, we are currently engaged in a study to determine whether we should formalize the relationship between administrative and academic computing and data management. Our effort is focused on determining the personnel and resource requirements that will be needed for the computing services at the college to remain current.

Randolph-Macon College

Randolph-Macon College is an independent liberal arts college for men and women. Founded in 1830, it continues to honor its historical relationship with the United Methodist Church. With an enrollment of approximately 1,000 students, the college has ninety-two faculty members and offers twenty-one majors.

The computer center presently has two Perkin-Elmer "super" minicomputers, one for academic use and one for administrative use. About 100 terminals and microcomputers are owned by the college. A Computer Literacy Program, begun in 1984, is required of all students and uses a computer classroom containing nineteen microcomputers.

The college has been aggressive in promoting the involvement of students and faculty in the use of computers in various ways. A National Science Foundation (NSF) grant in 1980 helped the college obtain its first state-of-the-art "super" minicomputer. Several workshops were held to train the faculty in the use of SPSS, computer interfacing, computer-aided instruction, and simple programming. A Jessie Ball duPont Foundation grant in 1983 helped faculty members purchase their own microcomputers. About 75 percent of the faculty took advantage of this opportunity, with the result that many faculty members now feel comfortable in using word processing, spreadsheet analysis, and database management programs. Many of the courses at the college presently use computers in some fashion to enhance the classroom experience.

The college joined OCLC and SOLINET in 1977, and all library materials acquired since then have been entered into the OCLC database. Funding will be needed in the near future for a retrospective conversion project to enter about 66,000 titles (books acquired before 1977) into the database. The library presently has one IBM XT microcomputer in addition to the OCLC M300 Workstation used with the OCLC system. A listing of serials holdings is produced for the library by the Computer Center. The library provides computer access to DIALOG and similar network services, allowing faculty and students to search national bibliographic databases.

A project to expand and renovate the library building is well under way and should be completed by December 1987. A well-equipped microcomputer room will include nineteen microcomputers for general use by students and faculty. The new library will be wired for extensive, diverse computer use and will provide the conduits, workstations, and other facilities which will be needed for possible future installation of library automation systems, expected to include an online public access catalog. Flexible participation by the library and its users in a campus computer network will be an important provision. During 1987–88 the library will prepare a long-range plan for library automation and seek funding for these needs.

The present network is one based upon RS-232 serial communication. Of the 100 or so terminals and microcomputers owned by the college, about 55 are connected to the two mainframe computers. Electronic mail and/or files can be sent between any two users of these terminals or microcomputers. Other microcomputers can access the two mainframe computers through dial-up modems. For now, the college is concentrating on providing each PC with its own software and a hard disk drive instead of using diskless microcomputers with a more powerful PC acting as a file server.

A major goal will be to provide easy access to the network for every person on campus. This should include providing a PC for each professor's office, clusters of microcomputers in the public areas of all academic buildings, and connections to the network in the dormitories for student-owned microcomputers. The rest of the microcomputers on campus, including other personally owned ones, will also be given access to the RS-232 network. Clusters of microcomputers, especially those in the Learning Center and in the new microcomputer room of the library, will be interconnected, using the RS-232 standard, to transfer files directly to each other as well as to communicate with the main computers on campus. The college will also be adding small "super" microcomputers to serve these clusters better. After prices come down considerably, the college will probably convert to a more powerful broadband or baseband network using fiber optics.

Union College

Union College is a primarily undergraduate, independent college that offers programs in engineering and computer science as well as the traditional liberal arts and sciences. Founded in 1779, Union established a tradition of emphasis on the synthesis of the liberal arts curriculum with contemporary science and technology that remains a unique characteristic of Union College today. Union's current enrollment is slightly more than 2,000 full-time undergraduates. An additional 300 students are enrolled part-time in graduate and continuing education, and there are 700 graduate students enrolled in engineering or management (mostly part-time). Union has 150 full-time and 30 part-time teaching faculty.

Union meets the needs of the academic computing community through a central facility, decentralized facilities linked to a campuswide network and stand-alone facilities. The central computing facility has five DEC VAX computers that may be accessed from approximately ninety terminals, microcomputers, and graphics workstations in public areas, and from a similar number of workstations utilized by faculty and administrators. Students may access the central cluster through these public facilities or from the 750 outlets available in dorm rooms connected to the network. The central cluster meets the electronic communication needs of the academic community, both on campus and off, through the use of various networks, including BITNET. The cluster also provides the tools to a group of faculty involved in writing courseware for a range of humanities courses. This year faculty from other divisions are being trained in the use of these tools.

Decentralized facilities linked to the network exist in Computer Science (VAX 11/750), Civil Engineering (MicroVAX II), and Social Sciences (MicroVAX II with twelve workstations). The Computer Science facility provides a UNIX environment for the more advanced students, as well as a research environment for faculty. The Civil Engineering facility allows this department to work on simulations critical to teaching and research in their discipline, and the Statistics Laboratory, located in the Social Sciences Division, permits faculty and students of this division to use statistical software in a dedicated environment. These three facilities are networked to the central facility through Ethernet technology. Eight of the nineteen departments on campus have their own microcomputer facilities, which has encouraged many faculty to incorporate the use of a microcomputer into their courses. The flexibility afforded academic departments in choosing the best equipment to meet their needs has contributed to the success of the decentralized facilities.

Union is committed to providing computing resources that can be utilized wherever the user works or lives. More resources are being decentralized, and this trend will continue. Decentralized departmental resources are better able to respond to specialized departmental needs. Additionally, there will be an increase in the use of microcomputers in the academic program, with the central facility's larger machines providing a hub for communications and database collections. As more work is done on microcomputers, the larger machines will become more available for larger tasks that utilize special software—in short, for things that really need to be done on larger machines. The thrust of the first long-range plan for computing at Union centered on hardware. The next planning will center on service and support, with emphasis on curricular issues.

Automation began in 1976 when the library started to use the OCLC system for cataloging. Through the efforts of a reclassification project begun in 1978, and a retrospective conversion project which began in October 1985, machine-readable records are available for approximately half of the collection, including most of the materials which circulate regularly. Book ordering at Schaffer Library was automated in 1983 through the OCLC Acquisitions Subsystem. Currently, the library is in the early stages of implementing an integrated library automation system, with the online public access catalog scheduled for release in fall 1987 and the circulation module in the next spring or summer [1988]. Data Research Associates has been selected as the software vendor. The system will run on a VAX 8250 that will be added to the VAX cluster on campus. This will integrate the system into the campus network, allowing easy access for anyone on the cluster, and will provide some backup for the library system should the VAX 8250 fail.

Union's computer network consists of components representing four technologies. The oldest of these is an RS-232 twisted-pair network connected to a Develcon Data Switch with approximately 500 incoming lines from student terminal clusters, faculty and administrative offices, micro labs, and classrooms. The data switch in turn connects to the academic cluster and the administrative computers. The second component is a four-segment Ethernet, connecting the Science and Engineering complex, the Social Science building, the Computer Science lab, and the library to the central cluster of five VAX computers. The third component is a fiber-optic network connecting 750 dorm rooms to the central cluster, controlled by Xyplex hardware. The fourth part is a pilot project which will transmit data over college-owned telephone lines, through an Intercom voice/data switch, to the Develcon.

Union's network covers almost the entire campus. Future expansion involves the establishment of more satellite facilities rather than wholesale expansion of the network itself. Addition of an Ethernet segment to accommodate the statistics laboratory and another in the library are examples of this. New terminals will be added using terminal servers on Ethernet, multiplexors on twisted pair, or data interfaces on telephone lines, depending on need and location. All offices and classrooms will eventually be connected to the network. We have decided to use the multimedia backbone to provide a structure on which we can build to provide new service.

University of Scranton

The University of Scranton is a small, comprehensive university which provides services to undergraduate, graduate, and nontraditional students in the Catholic, Jesuit, and liberal arts traditions. Founded in 1888 as Saint Thomas College by the Catholic bishop of the Scranton diocese, the university was administered for its first fifty years by the Brothers of the Christian Schools. In 1942 Scranton became the twenty-fourth higher educational institution in the United States operated by the Society of Jesus. The university has a total enrollment of approximately 4,800 (4,200 FTE) students in four colleges and schools: the College of Arts and Sciences, the School of Management, the Graduate School, and Dexter Hanley College for evening and adult learners. In fall 1987, a new College of Health, Education, and Human Resources became the fifth major academic division of the university. Of the full-time student population, about 70 percent are residential students.

Academic computing is supported by hardware which includes a DEC VAX 11/785 minicomputer, with eighty workstations, seven personal computer labs containing more than 100 IBM and AT&T personal computers, and a host of special devices including a Sun Microsystems workstation, a MicroVAX II with eight workstations, and microcomputers equipped for high-resolution graphics. Student and faculty users receive hands-on training and technical support from a staff of six full-time professionals, four graduate teaching assistants, and more than fifty trained work study students. Several computer labs are equipped for special computer instruction. Enhanced graphics projectors are installed in two facilities, while portable monochrome projectors can be signed out for classroom demonstrations.

Four years ago, the university initiated a successful faculty/staff microcomputer purchase program where the university subsidizes the purchase of IBM microcomputers for eligible faculty up to 40 percent of the total cost. This plan also includes a maintenance contract with an on-site Microcomputer Maintenance Center and a four-year, interest-free, payroll-deducted loan on the balance of the cost. A program to sell IBM microcomputers to students was initiated in fall 1986. The university offers students standard packages and options at discounts of up to 40 percent off list price. To date, more than 300 IBM personal computers have been sold to faculty, staff, and students.

Future areas of development in academic computing include the establishment of additional specialized labs for graphics, UNIX training, nursing, and journalism. DEC VAX distributed computing is expected to continue by utilizing the cluster options and DECnet with additional VAX workstations and MicroVAXs. Training programs will also be expanded and enhanced. Administrative computing is supported by an IBM 4341 computer utilizing a variety of terminals and, increasingly, IBM microcomputers and workstations.

The computing systems department is in the process of receiving approval for a major reorganization which brings all computing services together and organizes staff along functional lines, rather than the traditional academic and administrative lines. This process will also involve the gradual upgrading of staff positions and salaries over several years.

The improvement of hardware and software are continuing processes. The University of Scranton's most immediate need in this area is to upgrade the processor on the IBM mainframe, since the VAX was enhanced a year ago.

The university contracted with Geac Computers, Inc., in April 1986, for the installation of a computer-based bibliographic system. We are presently installing the following Geac modules: online circulation, materials acquisitions, full authority control, serials control, Boolean processing, online OCLC interface, and online public catalog. All modules are expected to be live by September 1987. We are now in the final stages of the installation of ALLAN (Alumni Memorial Library Local Area Network), which will become fully operational during summer 1987. ALLAN links all staff IBM PC workstations through ProNet/Novell NetWare for share-use of software and hardware. The library is cooperating with University Computing Systems in developing linkage between our Geac system and other external ProNet local area networks on the campus via a Geac-to-DEC VAX connection.

Longer-term developments for the library involve expansion of the physical plant, with the physical integration of the media resources operation into the library. The development of university archives with the aid of a state grant will also affect the physical plant situation in the next few years.

The university is currently involved with networking in two major areas, while exploring campuswide networking options. For telephone support, the university utilizes the Bell of Pennsylvania Centrex system. For PC cluster local area networks (LANs), the university has installed the ProNet network consisting of Proteon network components and the Novell Advanced NetWare 286 operating system. Five such cluster LANs are currently in operation in various locations supporting office systems and instructional/research needs. IBM ATs are utilized as file servers with disk capacities ranging from 20 megabytes to 160 megabytes per network. Hewlett-Packard laser printers and plotters are used as output devices on most cluster LANs.

Two alternatives are currently being explored to address a campuswide communications network. One possibility is to install a central switch on campus to handle data communications in both asynchronous and synchronous protocols. Both protocols are necessary because the university utilizes IBM mainframe hardware for administrative computing and DEC minicomputer hardware for academic computing. Voice and video communications could also be routed through a central switch. Obviously, this option would necessitate a wiring of the campus with either broadband or fiber-optic cable. The other option is to utilize the Bell of Pennsylvania central office switch to route data communications through existing telephone lines. Although only asynchronous protocols are currently supported directly, it is expected that synchronous protocols will soon be supported as well.

Currently, two electronic mail systems are in operation on campus. On the IBM mainframe, users utilize PROFS for electronic mail and scheduling facilities, while DEC VAX users utilize VAX Mail. There is now a connection between the systems that allows users to exchange mail. However, with the installation of the library Geac processor and the growth of standalone microcomputers and clusters on campus, there is a strong need to provide connectivity to multiple hosts and remote services such as BITNET. Thus, a campuswide communications system—technically, a complicated undertaking—is becoming a priority project.

Conference 2, November 8 – 9, 1987, Columbus, Ohio

Bradley University

Bradley University, located in Peoria, Illinois, was founded in 1897 as Bradley Polytechnic University. Since then, Bradley has become a four-year college and now a midsized university with 5,000 students, offering graduate programs and advanced degrees. Bradley offers twelve undergraduate degrees in sixty-three fields and thirteen graduate degrees in twenty-four fields through its five colleges: Business Administration, Communications and Fine Arts, Engineering and Technology, Liberal Arts and Science, and Education and Health Sciences.

Within the past two years, Bradley has advanced to a position of emerging leadership in information technology. We have expanded mainframe and departmental computing capability, networked the campus for voice, data and video distribution, placed hundreds of personal computers in residence halls and faculty and administrative offices, constructed new computer laboratories, and launched innovative new information technology projects, an example of which is our Admissions Office of the Future.

The goals underlying the development of our campus information system are these:

- To enhance and support our academic programs;
- To facilitate effective and efficient institutional operation and informed decision making;
- To provide advanced information processing tools to students, faculty, and administrators;
- To position Bradley University as a high-quality information-intensive university;
- To provide universal voice connectivity between students, staff, faculty and administrators, and data connectivity between these groups and all available computing and information resources, both on and off campus; and
- To unify delivery of voice, data, and video services.

Academic computing is accomplished on a range of facilities. A new university mainframe computer—a Control Data Cyber 180-830—was installed in January 1986, and has since been supplemented with eight departmental multiuser computing systems. Students are provided personal and class accounts on the Cyber mainframe and departmental minicomputers, and plentiful system resources are made available. Over the past two or three years, microcomputers have proliferated on campus, having achieved highest penetration in the Colleges of Business and Engineering, with Communications and Arts gaining rapidly. During the past two academic years, several new laboratory facilities were completed, including the doubling in size of a business computer lab and the addition of new laboratories for computer science and the English department's composition program.

An innovative microcomputer project for students was launched in fall 1986 called the "Residence Hall of the Future" project. In this project, residence hall rooms were provided with complete microcomputer systems, including an AT&T Model 6300 PC, professional word processing, spreadsheet, graphics and communications software, a printer, and a high-speed connection to the campuswide communication network. This project has grown rapidly, and now involves two residence halls and nearly 600 students, encompassing 45 percent of the incoming freshman class. To provide general student access to microcomputers, PC clusters have been established in the library, the Computer Center, and in other convenient locations. The Residence Hall of the Future project has produced a number of positive side effects, including increased enrollment. The project has helped contribute to a 1986 increase in freshman enrollment of 17 percent, and a 1987 increase of the same magnitude.

A second effect has been to generate faculty involvement. Because of the large number of students participating in the project, many faculty noted that students in their classes had achieved a significant degree of information-processing ability. This, in turn, led faculty to seek access to a PC and the network. This fall, in answer to these requests, the university has sponsored a "microcomputers for faculty" program. Full-time faculty may apply for the loan of a university-acquired PC package including software and a network connection. The university further supports faculty and staff computing through low-cost subsidized loans for the purchase of computing equipment and software.

One year ago, Bradley became an electronically unified campus, with the completion of a new telephone system, a fiber-optic-based data communication network (an AT&T Information Systems Network, ISN), and an upgraded CCTV network. Now, voice, data, and video services are available to every residence hall room, office, and laboratory. During the first twelve months the network was in place, 76 percent growth in the number of network connections was experienced.

All workstations, terminals, and host processors are accessible through the campus network. In addition, incoming and outgoing modem pools facilitate external access to the network, and permit on-net access to distant databases.

Several buildings have internal AppleTalk and Starlan networks, linking clusters of microcomputers. Future networking plans include the development of a high-speed backbone network based on Ethernet and TCP/IP for interprocessor communication.

The library's circulation and catalog systems are fully automated, and in September [1987], access to the online catalog was made available campuswide through the data network. The library also provides the Infotrac periodicals index on CD-ROM, access to the OCLC system, and free access to online database searches.

The library has been active in automation efforts for more than five years. Circulation and the public access catalog are completely automated, and the library closed the card catalog in August 1986.

A major expansion of the library is projected to begin this spring, doubling the available space to house the collection, and providing a significant increase in study space for students and research space for faculty and graduate students.

The College of Wooster

An independent liberal arts college, the College of Wooster currently enrolls some 1,800 students and has a faculty FTE of 157. The college's curriculum includes a required freshman program, optional sophomore-level interdisciplinary seminars, well-defined majors, and a required junior- and senior-year research and thesis project (known as "Independent Study").

Wooster is in the process of evolving from central, college-owned computing facilities to distributed, mixed-ownership systems. The central academic computing system consists of two clustered VAX 11/750 computers, each with 14 megabytes of memory and sharing one gigabyte of disk. There are thirty-two communications ports on each machine for a total of sixty-four ports. Forty ports are connected to a broadband local area network. The remaining twenty-four ports are directly connected to terminals in the Academic Computing Center. There are about seventy additional terminals across the campus in residence halls, common rooms, and faculty offices. We are running DEC's standard VAX/VMS operating system, slightly reduced for student access, which is through course-related accounts. There is a bulletin board and an electronic mail system available on the VAX. There are about 250 personal computers on campus, and the number is increasing by about 80 each year. About one-third of the personal computers are college-owned, while the remainder belong to students and faculty. About two-thirds of the personal computers are Apple Macintoshes, and the remainder are a mixed bag. The college is a (nonprofit) reseller of the Apple Macintosh equipment.

The Computer Center includes a microcomputer laboratory with eight Macintoshes, seven Apple IIes, ten DEC Rainbows, and two IBM microcomputers. Laser and draft printers are available for both the VAXs and the Macintoshes; draft and letter-quality printers for the other machines. A microcomputer software library and student consulting services are available in the Center. There are about twenty personal computers available to students in residence halls, the student center, and the academic departments. At present, it appears that personal computers are used mainly for word processing, while the central facilities provide for the more traditional computing needs: statistical analyses, computer programming, and research data processing of various kinds. The Academic Computer Center additionally provides some computing support to the college library for databases and bibliographies.

With the completion of the retrospective conversion of all Library of Congress materials, the library is ready to move forward in planning for an online catalog. We will continue adding our extensive collection of government documents to the OCLC database. During the next several months, guidelines describing our specific criteria for each mode of an integrated online catalog will be discussed and written. At the same time, attention will be given to the variety of systems presently available, developing technology, and the level of support that the systems would require from the Computer Center. A recommendation should go forward during the spring concerning implementation and funding needs for such a program.

Wooster installed a broadband cable network on campus in April 1983. That system continues to provide digital communications and educational television broadcasting to residence halls and academic buildings. There are local AppleTalk networks in four residence halls and one academic building. Each AppleTalk network has required some additional wiring in the building. There is an IBM PC network in the psychology department. All of the AppleTalk networks include a laser printer; two include file service with a 20 megabyte disk. The broadband cable provides communications with the central computing system; the AppleTalk and IBM networks are limited to individual residence halls and the single department. None of these networks involves more than twenty personal computers. Since the current campuswide broadband network is not Ethernet-based, we are in the process of identifying affordable alternatives to interconnect the AppleTalk networks, and to give them access to the central computing system. Fewer than one-fourth of the personal computers on campus are connected to any network. Some students, faculty, and administrators have discussed external networks such as BITNET, but there does not appear to be a consensus about the value of these systems on our campus.

We will be planning our next steps in each of these areas in the next twelve to eighteen months.

Earlham College

Located in Richmond, Indiana, Earlham is a four-year, liberal arts college which currently enrolls about 1,000 students on campus, with another seventy on foreign study programs at any one time. Earlham's Quaker heritage leads it to emphasize cooperative learning by our students and deemphasize the competitive model of academic achievement.

Currently, Earlham relies on both mainframes and microcomputers for campus academic computing. Our Computing Center—located in Lilly Library—houses two VAX 11/750s connected with DECnet. The heaviest use by students is word processing; at present, we have slightly more than 800 active accounts which are used for this purpose each term. The VAXs also support advanced computer science courses, a large statistical package (SPSS-X), and occasional heavy number-crunching by members of the physics and chemistry departments. Programming languages available to academic users include Pascal, FORTRAN, BASIC, LISP, ICON, FORTH, and VAX MACRO-II.

Time-sharing terminals, connected to the mainframes, are available in most academic buildings. At present, there are forty-four of these terminals available to students and faculty in public areas. All through the term, ten of the forty-four terminals are made available to students twenty-four hours a day. In addition, during the last two weeks of each term, a second group of ten terminals can be used on an around-the-clock basis.

In fall 1985, IBM gave the college a twenty-five-station IBM PC Lab in return for further developing DELPHI—a program that allows students to carry on a structured review of course materials and present each other with discussion questions that grow directly out of the events and readings in a course. This PC Lab is used regularly for DELPHI development but also supports some introductory programming courses and a growing amount of microcomputer word processing.

In addition to the terminals and microcomputers mentioned, there is a heterogeneous cluster of microcomputers in the Computing Center. The main purposes of this cluster are to facilitate file transfer between differing machines and to provide printing facilities for students who have their own microcomputers but have difficulty affording their own printer. The machines in the cluster—an Apple IIe, three Macintoshes, and an IBM PC—are networked together via low-speed RS-232 ports to allow file transfer from one type of machine to another. In addition, any of these microcomputers can be used to move text files to and from the college VAXs. Finally, through the network, all these machines have access to dot matrix printing (as well as laser printing in the case of the Macintoshes). Besides file transfer, the cluster is used heavily for desktop publishing and the output of graphics materials to the laser printers.

Most academic departments have microcomputers as needed for student use and for departmental word processing and administrative purposes. The variety of users is wide. For example, math and physics maintain a cluster of twelve Apple IIs which are primarily available to their students for programming and lab exercises. The music department uses an Apple II with add-on hardware to teach pitch recognition. Sports and movement studies have a setup that allows the graphic analysis of the human body in motion. Geology uses two machines for computer-aided instruction. Psychology and biology use their microcomputers for light-duty, user-friendly statistical processing.

The campus information strategy can be stated simply: have a single administrative database, but supply administrative offices with adequate hardware and training to access this database directly, with minimal reliance on professional Computing Center staff.

Earlham uses the relational database ORACLE and is nearing the point at which administrative information from offices as varied as admissions, financial aid, the registrar, student development, accounting, and alumni development is maintained by ORACLE and is available on a decentralized basis to those offices with a need for it. ORACLE has an easy-to-learn query language and once the data has been entered, many query tasks, and all updating of the database, are easily carried out by administrative office staff.

Lilly Library uses microcomputers in a number of ways. First of all, as members of OCLC, our technical services staff uses two M300 Workstations for cataloging and interlibrary lending. Secondly, we use our own microcomputers (one in Lilly Library and one in the Science Library) and a DECmate II for a variety of reference functions: online searching (by both staff and end-users), record keeping, storing, producing and updating bibliographies, and word processing for correspondence and reports.

Finally, we use microcomputing to provide access to our CD-ROMs. In the main library there are two microcomputers with CD-ROM drives; in the Science Library, we have one PC and one CD-ROM drive. All have printers attached. In the past year we have moved a long way toward substituting the use of CD-ROMs for online database searching. We expect this trend to continue and even go further; CD-ROMs will become an increasingly important means of providing information.

Over the next five years we look forward to two main changes: increased connectivity of all computers on campus and the increasing spread of personally owned microcomputers among our students.

In the short run, connectivity will come first at the local level, since we intend to aid administrative work groups and academic departments to set up simple low-speed local area networks (LANs). Currently, the Computing Center staff is experimenting with a heterogeneous LAN which supports both IBM microcomputers and Apple machines on AppleTalk. The LAN (called TOPS) allows file transfer and laser printing by Macintoshes and IBM microcomputers. Because we are using existing cable pairs available in previously installed phone cable, we expect that we will be able to put LANs in place with a minimum of effort.

The next stage will be to build gateways from the LANs to DECnet and the mainframe. Given new technology which allows using existing phone cabling for 10 megabyte Ethernet connections, we expect that this too will be possible with a minimum of rewiring on campus.

There is considerable likelihood that Lilly Library will purchase its own VAX to do administrative tasks and maintain an online catalog. Through DECnet, this catalog could be made available at all academic and administrative terminals and eventually at all microcomputers on campus.

To date, as is the case at similar institutions, we have not seen an explosion of computer ownership among our students. Currently, no more than 10 percent of them come to campus with computers. However, we still expect the explosion to come, and plan to be ready for it. Here again, we anticipate relying on the phone system for connectivity. Personal phone lines are spreading in the dorms, and we are exploring ways to utilize these lines as a means of giving students occasional access to the main computing hub on campus.

Thus, in the long run, we expect to keep one VAX running in parallel to serve as the communications hub for campus computing activity and to support the administrative database. Increasingly, we expect word processing, programming, and CAI to migrate to microcomputers which will have access, as needed, to the VAX hub over the networks described.

Kalamazoo College

Kalamazoo College is a private, residential liberal arts college serving a student body of 1,200 full-time students. The student to faculty ratio is 14:1. The college has a broad-based curriculum leading to the B.A. degree, with twenty-two majors and more than a dozen other areas of concentration. In the Kalamazoo Plan, students alternate on-campus classroom and cocurricular activities with off-campus experiences such as internships, foreign study, and the senior independent project. The college also offers a new program in international education.

Kalamazoo College offers a computer science major and several supporting courses in mathematics and physics. More than one-third of each year's class enrolls in a computer science course. In addition, there are about thirty courses in various departments in which students use the computer. Usage studies indicate that in any given term, 90 percent of the students on campus use the central computing system. The primary educational computing facility is a Digital VAX 11/750 superminicomputer serving a campus network of forty-six terminals, several hard-wired microcomputers, and five dial-up ports for off-campus users.

The use of microcomputers for educational computing is rapidly expanding here as elsewhere. In addition to those used regularly in the sciences, mathematics, educational computing, psychology, philosophy, education and music, a plan for clusters of microcomputers for general use is currently being implemented.

In addition to the campus network, the VAX also serves as the gateway to ZOONET, a local area network that links the computing facilities of the member institutions of the Kalamazoo Consortium of Higher Education. It is through this link that Kalamazoo College is also joined with the MERIT Network, a statewide network linking computing facilities at the public educational institutions of Michigan. Resources beyond Michigan are reached through Telenet or similar services. The VAX terminals are distributed across the campus in student clusters and faculty and staff office areas.

The library has been working toward fully automated operations since it first joined OCLC in 1974. Conversion of all its cataloging was completed in 1984, and the staff is currently in the final stage of planning for a full, integrated library automation system, a project sponsored by the Pew Memorial Trust. The planned connection of the library system with the educational computing system will provide campuswide access to the library's bibliographic information, while network connections will link our catalog and our users with other local libraries as well as with academic libraries throughout the state. The library also offers, as an active and growing component of its reference service and bibliographic instruction program, the national online information services of DIALOG, BRS, Chemical Abstracts, and others.

Kenyon College

Kenyon College, located in rural Gambier, Ohio, is a liberal arts institution with approximately 1,550 undergraduate students and 120 faculty members. Founded in 1824, Kenyon is the oldest still-private trans-Appalachian college in the United States. It honors historical ties with the Episcopal Church but is nonsectarian by principle.

Kenyon's academic computing program is still relatively modest: only about 25 percent of the faculty and students use college computing facilities each week. However, the college aspires to have a program comparable to those at the best liberal arts colleges, and it is entering a period of significant growth and development in computing. The college recently built a new library which included office space and a new VAX 8600 system for Academic Computing Services. About fifty terminals scattered around the campus are attached to the VAX 8600 system. A cluster of networked Leading Edge microcomputers, a VAX 11/730 system, and a variety of printers and plotters provide additional hardware resources.

Kenyon is beginning to automate its new library and is proceeding with specific plans, worked out during the past year, to complete the task during the next two years. Accordingly, a contract has been signed for the retrospective conversion to machine-readable tape of library's holdings; the process will begin during the winter. The library staff will issue an RFP (request for proposal) for library hardware and software this fall and anticipates negotiating a contract in late spring. A committee is currently conducting a search for a systems specialist who will work with both library and Computer Center staff to install and eventually to manage the system. Barring disasters, the college hopes to be fully automated by the beginning of 1989–90.

The college is also attentive to the need to increase linkages among the various computer islands on the campus. The data communications system that connects the terminals to the VAX time-sharing systems uses dedicated, college-owned twisted-pair wires and leased telephone lines. While the present system is rather primitive, the college is embarking on a three-year plan to improve access to computing. During the past summer, new data wiring was installed in the main classroom/office building; and the first links of a complete campus network will eventually be extended to the library, the residence halls, and all offices, laboratories, studios, and classrooms. The number of terminals available to students will be doubled and workstations will be installed in almost all faculty offices. Kenyon does not currently belong to any national electronic mail systems, but there is strong interest in joining BITNET.

In summary, Kenyon is proceeding on four fronts. (1) An expansion of student access is under way; and while the college has not yet decided the optimum ratio of workstations to students, it is clear that more terminals or microcomputers are currently in order. (2) An expansion of faculty access is simultaneously under way, with the goal of making an appropriately configured workstation available to every faculty member who chooses to have one. (3) The automation of the library is under way; when completed, the system will bring the catalog online and revolutionize procedures for acquisitions and accounting. (4) Finally, the wiring of the campus is under way, and we expect within a few years to have the kind of connectivity that will allow us to maximize the value of our resources.

Knox College

Knox College is a nonsectarian liberal arts college of a thousand students and eighty faculty members. Its mission is to offer each of its students a challenging liberal education. Knox emphasizes undergraduate research, culminating for some seniors in honors projects that are then evaluated by outside examiners.

The college offers general courses in computer science and a major as well. A DEC PDP 11/44 timesharing system is used in computer science instruction, as well as to provide computing support for courses in the natural and social sciences. Word processing capability is provided on the timesharing system and by publicly available Apple Macintosh computers in the main and science libraries. Additional microcomputers (Macintosh, Apple II/GS, IBM-compatible and CP/M based) are located in several departments. A majority of the faculty own personal computers, due in large part to an interest-free loan program established to encourage faculty computer usage. Many of these faculty have introduced the computer as an important tool in their courses, either through commercial software or programs which have been locally developed.

All the cataloging and most of the interlibrary loan requests in the Knox College Library are handled on OCLC system. Our acquisitions are automated, using a program designed by our data processing department that operates on the college's mainframe. Database searching is done exclusively on DIALOG. Serials control is in the primary stages of being automated, using a microcomputer and commercial software. A project for cross-referencing an extensive archives is at a similar stage using similar tools.

Aside from the network of timesharing terminals, there is a small AppleTalk network for accessing an Apple LaserWriter printer. An internal network is being planned to interconnect the many microcomputers and allow access from these machines to the central timesharing system. In addition, Knox anticipates connecting to the BITNET network operated by EDUCOM.

The college is on the brink of a major investment in computers. Some of the hardware decisions have already been made. Raising funds for further investment is an important aspect of the college's newly launched capital campaign. The college is currently exploring a library circulation scheme using microcomputers, and it is eager to provide remote access to the library catalog as well. Plans are well along for a statistics lab, a VAX that will be totally dedicated to computer science and computer-based courses in calculus and chemistry. In addition, planning is well under way to complete the computerization of the admissions and development operations. The college is now searching for a faculty member in computer science, whose appointment will mean a net increase of faculty in that department.

Loyola University

Founded in 1912, Loyola University in New Orleans is a Catholic institution that revolves around the Jesuit tradition of contributing to the liberal education of the whole person. Loyola is a medium-sized university with a total enrollment of approximately 5,200 students. The university offers fifty bachelor degree programs and twelve masters programs through its College of Arts and Sciences, College of Business Administration, College of Music, and City College. A Juris Doctor program is available through the School of Law. Faculty to student ratio varies from 1:5 in music to 1:18 in business.

Students have access to approximately 115 microcomputers and thirty-four printers throughout the campus. Five labs (two located in classroom buildings, two in residence halls, and one in the library's Media Center) are available for general student use and five additional labs support special programs in writing across the curriculum, intensive English, math basic skills, English basic skills, and The Maroon (student newspaper). Of the 115 systems, 25 percent are IBM-compatibles, 45 percent are Macintoshes, and 30 percent are of the Apple II family.

A variety of microcomputers are to be found in faculty and department offices throughout the campus. Several departments, such as mathematics, business administration, and the College of Arts and Sciences, have dedicated faculty labs with microcomputers sharing printers on local area networks.

The School of Law, located on the Broadway Campus, has both a Novell and a 3-Com local area network linking more than thirty-six IBM-compatibles in faculty offices, student labs, and the Poverty Law Clinic. These networks provide students and faculty access to legal word processing software and a client database.

The Loyola Micro Center provides significant discounts to students, faculty, and staff on name brand computers, peripherals, and software. The Micro Center currently sells Apple, IBM, Zenith, and Packard Bell computer systems. Weekly training courses, laser printing, microcomputer repairs, and other support services are provided. Sales for 1987/88 are projected to exceed $700,000.

A Hewlett-Packard 3000 minicomputer supports forty-eight ports, has 3 megabytes of memory, and 400 megabytes of disk storage. In addition to compilers for BASIC, COBOL, FORTRAN, and Pascal, the Hewlett-Packard 3000 supports the instructional program with a line-oriented text editor (QEDit), two text formatters (Galley and Prose), mathematics modeling software, and statistics programs including SPSS-X and Minitab.

A DEC VAX 11/750 supports thirty-two external ports, has 8 megabytes of memory, and two 120 megabyte hard disk drives. Its compilers include ADA, BASIC, C, FORTRAN, Pascal, and a macro-assembler. It has two page oriented editors (EMACS and EDIT) and a text formatting program (RUNOFF). In addition, the VAX also has programs for statistics (SPSS-X), symbolic manipulation and differential equations (MAXSYMA), graphics (PLOT 10), and several marketing and business simulations programs.

A Gandalf PACX 4 data switch is used to connect terminals to both of the two minicomputer systems. With the exception of a small cluster of terminals in psychology which are connected directly to the Hewlett-Packard 3000, all terminals on campus are connected through this switch. Student access to the minicomputers is primarily obtained through the Terminal Lab in Monroe Hall. This area houses eighteen terminals and two line printers which are available seven days a week. Several small clusters or terminals exist in the student union and two residence halls, as well. Several faculty and department offices throughout the campus are equipped with terminals. In addition, eight dial-up lines are installed in the PACX data switch to accommodate remote users.

Loyola University Library uses the OCLC system for acquiring and cataloging books and for interlibrary loan. In spring 1987, the library began an upgrade of its CLSI circulation system and by the spring of 1988 plans to have implemented an online catalog. The library reference staff provide online searching through DIALOG, BRS, and other database vendors and provide opportunity for faculty and students to do their own database searches using Infotrac and Wilsonline.

Because of limited funds, current academic computing needs are not satisfied. Yet, it is likely that the need for computing access will increase as the university community becomes more computer aware and literate. A long-range plan for academic computing services is currently being developed to help solve this critical problem. Academic Computing Services is planning for a major upgrade to the minicomputer systems and is hopeful that it can be funded in 1988/89.

In the future, the library must upgrade its OCLC hardware to accommodate the new OCLC Online System. Plans are also being made to provide terminals for public access to the OCLC Online Union Catalog. In addition, the library hopes to expand the number of terminals and to add such activities as acquisitions and serials control to the system. As a means of expanding access to bibliographic and other databases, the library is exploring purchase of indexes on CD-ROM. The library is looking forward to the day when the campus telecommunications network will be in place, providing students and faculty access from their offices or residence halls to a variety of online information resources.

Rosary College

Rosary College, incorporated in 1901 and located in a residential suburb of Chicago, is a comprehensive educational institution composed of undergraduate and graduate divisions. It is small, Catholic, and coeducational. The college offers liberal arts and professional education through a variety of disciplines. Its undergraduate programs serve 631 full-time and 275 part-time students, of whom about 300 are residents. The three graduate schools—library and information science, business, and special education—enroll about 636 students, giving a current headcount of 1,542 and an FTE enrollment of 982. There are 123 faculty members who are weighted as 87 FTE faculty. This produces an FTE student faculty ratio of 11:1.

Academic computing at Rosary encompasses not only the traditional computer science courses but also utilization of computers in a variety of liberal arts courses and academic library functions. These activities are supported by one centrally located computer lab, three smaller satellite laboratories, and the library. The central computer lab is open and staffed with trained assistants for nearly ninety hours per week. A variety of personal computers including fourteen Apples and thirty-six MS-DOS based units, twenty-one dot matrix printers, one laser printer and twenty-six terminals (eighteen CRTs and eight printer terminals), supporting academic programs, are distributed throughout these locations. In addition, Rosary has communication equipment which permits thirteen of the CRTs (eleven administrative, two academic), nine microcomputers (one administrative, eight academic), and two high-speed line printers to link directly to Concordia College's mainframe computers. Concordia College, a neighboring liberal arts institution, has a powerful and versatile cluster of three Digital Equipment Corporation computers and an excellent professional staff to support our administrative and academic computing needs on a contract basis.

Rosary College Library has used the OCLC system for cataloging library materials, for interlibrary loan, and for instruction in the Graduate School of Library and Information Science since 1976. Library staff used OCLC-developed PC software program, MICROCON®, for a recent retrospective conversion and the magnetic tapes of cataloging records have been used to create the Library Computer System (LCS) database. Rosary Library went online in August 1987. Participation in LCS, a network of twenty-nine Illinois academic libraries providing shared computer circulation files and, soon, an online catalog, has greatly expanded resources available to faculty and students. The library houses approximately 180,000 books; the network makes nine million available through reciprocal borrowing. Other functions which rely on information technology include a CD-ROM for *Books-in-Print,* online searching of indexes through DIALOG, and the transmission of documents via telefacsimile equipment.

Currently, no formal computer networks are in place at Rosary. However, administrative users have the capability of interacting by sharing institutional databases on the DEC cluster of Concordia. Most of the hardware on campus is compatible, so a network in the future could be easily implemented.

Faculty will continue to be encouraged to integrate computers into the curriculum. A program is being developed introducing all freshman to traditional library research techniques and new automated information resources, and requiring them to use word processing in class work. Plans are being developed for a computer equipped classroom to serve these needs. The library needs to examine the automation of acquisitions and serials functions, and to expand student and faculty use of computerized information sources. End user searching of computerized indexes is under consideration. Next summer [1988] we hope to label the circulating collection with OCR (optical character recognition) labels to facilitate circulation. A small network is being considered which will permit cost effective utilization of expensive software programs such as PC-based SPSS-X.

Conference 3, February 22-23, 1988, Pomona, California

Grinnell College

Founded in 1846, Grinnell College is a private, nondenominational institution with an average enrollment of 1,250 students and a faculty-student ratio of 1:11.4. The humanities, social sciences, sciences, and special programs comprise the basic curriculum. Grinnell also offers pre-professional training in medicine, architecture, law, and engineering, and more than forty-five off-campus programs in the U.S. and abroad.

Academic computing at Grinnell is based on DEC VAX computers and peripheral equipment and several micro/workstation networks. Those in academic computing have access to a VAX 8600 and two VAX 11/750s that are arranged in a VAX cluster. Access to the VAX computer is through a Micom switch. All faculty and staff are provided with desktop connections to the VAX. DEC terminals and microcomputers are available in ten public terminal rooms. Public printers are available to students and faculty and include dot-matrix as well as laser printers. Computer Services employs five programmer/analysts, a systems manager, and a manager of educational services for consultation with faculty, students, and administrative staff.

Computer Services provides instruction on computing for new students to Grinnell at the beginning of the semester. The "Introduction to Computing and Text Processing" workshops are taught primarily by student user consultants. Approximately 60 percent of the new students in the fall of 1987 attended these workshops. All students are assigned computer accounts upon matriculation at Grinnell. These accounts and virtually unlimited usage are free to students. Approximately 85 percent of students use computers on a regular basis for their academic work.

Computer use is also integrated into the curriculum in a number of areas that are not traditionally computer intensive, including the arts, music, Chinese, and others.

Faculty research involves the computer in a number of ways, including uses in text database applications in the humanities, real-time analyses of experimental data and lab interfacing in psychology and chemistry, computer-controlled data-gathering and telescope orientation in astronomy, computer-aided design in the visual arts, simulation and modelling in the natural and social sciences, MIDI interfaces and desktop publishing of musical scores in music, and so on. Faculty are also regular users of such facilities as the ICPSR data sets and BITNET/Internet.

Grinnell has no network in the library. We make extensive use of computing in the library, however. Ten years ago, our library began to catalog books using the OCLC system. Since then, all new cataloging has been done on the OCLC system, and the entire collection has been converted. At present, Grinnell has approximately 200,000 records in machine-readable form. We plan to add an online catalog as soon as possible.

Our library uses the SC350, OCLC's microcomputer-based automated serials control system. Bibliographic database searches are offered through DIALOG, BRS, and other database vendors. An OCLC terminal is available to students and faculty.

A Micom 600 data switch has provided Grinnell College with minimal network functionality since 1983.

Each of our 600 terminals and personal computers, located in various buildings, is able to access any of four central minicomputers. Additionally, our four VAXs operate in a Digital VAX cluster which allows storage media and printers to be shared among all of the VAX computers.

Grinnell is in the initial stages of building a campuswide high-speed Ethernet network which will allow resource sharing and high-speed data transmission among all campus computers. This past summer, we installed the first fiber-optic connection between the Computer Services building and a newly constructed addition to the Science Building. Thirty-eight Sun workstations, twenty Compaq computers, and our VAX cluster are connected to this network. We have plans to extend this high-speed network to all campus buildings during the next four years.

Lewis and Clark College

Lewis and Clark College is a small, private institution with a liberal arts and sciences undergraduate college at its core, that offers selective graduate programs in professional studies and a comprehensive education in law. The undergraduate curriculum consists of twenty-eight majors and twenty-six minors housed in twenty-two academic departments. Approximately 1,800 of the total student FTE of 2,700 are undergraduates. The total instructional faculty FTE is 200, of which 111 FTE reside in the undergraduate college of arts and sciences. The average student to faculty ratio at the undergraduate level is 14:1.

During the early 1980s, the institution experienced a rapid and generally uncoordinated growth of microcomputer technology and library automation on campus. The institution created an undergraduate program in computer science, largely service-oriented but offering a minor in computer science. With the assistance of a grant from the Apple Corporation, the first-year Core Curriculum course was restructured to include Macintosh computers as a central tool of writing and critical thinking. Selected academic departments, e.g., business and administrative studies, initiated the integration of computers throughout their curricula. Lewis and Clark currently has more than eighty Macintosh systems in open labs which are available twenty-four hours a day for student use. The majority of Macs are located in clusters in the dormitories, and the resident assistants to the dormitories play an active role in instructing students new to the system. In addition to the Macintoshes, more than two dozen IBM-compatible clones are available on twenty-four-hour access in several locations. Academic computing not only provides direct support for computing applications in courses, but provides computing support to the student government and the student newspaper, as well.

To date, the Watzek Library has followed an incremental approach to automation, using microcomputers selectively to assist in technical and business functions. The principal thrust of library automation to this point has been development of online access to various bibliographic databases. The library funds all electronic searches by students, faculty, and staff without restriction. In addition, the library was funded direct end-user searching in one department (Chemistry) and has plans to extend to two more departments. In combination with the online searching, the library is a full member of OCLC and a dial-access member of WLN and RLG. Currently, three different local area networks are being evaluated on campus.

As a result of our 1986–87 planning process, several decisions have been made about the future of academic computing and library automation for the institution. First, we have made the strategic decision to create and implement a program of computing-across-the-curriculum instead of upgrading undergraduate computer science to the status of a full academic major. Conceived to parallel the institution's program of writing-across-the-curriculum, this program reflects Lewis and Clark's commitment to computing and information technologies as central tools of knowledge retrieval, transmission, and creation pervasive throughout all disciplines of study. Further, we have chosen not to define computing-across-the-curriculum as a standard "computer literacy" course; rather, we are striving for the discipline-specific integration of computing and information technologies throughout all departments of study.

Second, we have dismantled the Office of Computing Services which housed both academic and administrative computing under the direction of a single director. The institution now has a single director of the Library and Academic Computing, and a separate Office of Information Services to handle administrative computing. The strategic decision to link the library with academic computing reflects the institution's view that the library, like writing and computing, is a tool of knowledge, and we are seeking a creative and innovative merger of library and information technologies. The institution has recently formed a Computing Planning Committee to develop the institution's master plan for academic and administrative computing in the next three to five years.

Loyola Marymount University

Loyola Marymount University (LMU), located in Los Angeles, is a Catholic coeducational university following the educational traditions of the Jesuits and the Religious of the Sacred Heart of Mary. Loyola's undergraduate program centers around four colleges, each containing specialized programs to meet the interests of a diverse student population. LMU has an undergraduate population of 3,700 and a faculty of 240. There are graduate programs offered on the Westchester campus enrolling more than 1,000 students each semester. The Loyola Law School, the tenth largest in the country, is located on a downtown campus.

In terms of developing an integrated campuswide information system, we are at the thinking and early planning stages. We are ready to issue Requests for Proposals for both a voice/data PBX system and an integrated automation system for the library.

Our library joined OCLC in 1981, using the network's cataloging module. At that time, the library changed from the Dewey to the Library of Congress classification system. This fall, the library finished converting all of its Dewey materials to the LC system, again using the OCLC Online System in preparation for having an online public catalog. Online database searching began for the faculty in 1984. We are planning on making this service available to students this coming spring. This year the library is experimenting with two compact disc indexing systems that duplicate heavily used paper services to which we subscribe. The staff is investigating the cost/benefit of compact disc systems vs. paper-based services.

Last year, a library committee developed specifications for an integrated automation system to handle an online public catalog, acquisitions, serials control, and circulation. We expect to issue an RFP for such a system sometime this spring. Library staff are currently using eleven microcomputers for word processing and database management activities. These computers will interface with any library automation system we acquire. We have also ordered four of the OCLC M310® Workstations, two with hard disks, which will help us control our networking costs.

The present state of academic computing is good. Student on-campus access to micro-, mini-, and mainframe computers has greatly improved in the last few years. The Colleges of Business and Science and Engineering have their own microcomputer laboratories. There are three other university laboratories dedicated to general purpose computing including word processing. These labs are staffed by professional managers who are assisted by word-study students. Overall, there is about one computer workstation for every twenty-five undergraduates. Support for faculty computing, beyond sharing resources with students, needs improvement. There are two small faculty computing labs; however, most faculty want to have a microcomputer in their offices. To date, the University has provided office microcomputers to about one-fifth of the faculty. Several faculty have also purchased a microcomputer for home use through interest-free loans provided by the university.

The present state of networking on campus is primitive. With a few minor exceptions, all computer workstations are centralized or stand-alone. There are no high-speed microcomputer networks or digital networks of any kind. Remote access to the university mainframe and minicomputers is by low-speed dial-up modem through our present Pac-Bell CENTREX telephone system and its associated twenty-year-old cable plant.

Our plans to expand academic computing are directly linked to our plans to develop campus communications and networking. We are currently in the RFP evaluation stage of a project to replace all of our campus telephone cables and install a PBX capable of switching moderate-speed data. We anticipate installing extra cable to support high-speed digital networks and video in the future. As part of this project, we are also considering the provision of data services to all dorm rooms. It is anticipated that achieving campuswide connectivity will only increase the demand for computer services. As a result, a larger mainframe will be installed to act as the hub of the academic data network, and more microcomputers will be obtained for faculty and students to take advantage of the improved connectivity.

Mills College

Founded in 1852, Mills is the oldest women's college in the United States. A small, independent institution in the San Francisco Bay area, the college enrolls approximately 1,050 students each year. In 1987–88, the student body consisted of 810 women undergraduates and 246 graduate men and women students. There are seventy-two full-time faculty members and eighty-two part-time, with an overall faculty FTE of approximately ninety-nine. The college has a student-to-faculty ratio of 9.3:1. Mills offers the B.A. degree, providing a choice of thirty-three undergraduate majors and an option for students to design interdisciplinary "college majors." At the graduate level, the college offers the M.A. and the M.F.A. in a limited number of fields as well as a variety of teaching credential programs.

Since 1960, the college has offered courses using computing, and in 1974 was the first small liberal arts college in the nation to establish a computer science major. Since 1979, residence halls have contained terminals connected to the academic minicomputer for student use, and more recently Macintoshes have been added to each residence hall's computer room. Since 1982, the growth trends in academic computing at Mills have been shifting away from centralized computing on the academic VAX minicomputer and toward a model of distributed computing involving microcomputers. The annual number of VAX users has increased at a rate of only 10 percent while the annual known number of academic microcomputers has increased by approximately 670 percent. The majority of these users now work at campus locations other than the Academic Computing Center and the Computer Learning Studio, where professional staff are located. In the same timeframe, the number of college-owned terminals, printers, and microcomputers for academic computing has increased by 585 percent and the number of known user-owned terminals and microcomputers by 2,960 percent. During 1986–87, thirty-nine faculty members in seventeen disciplines offered seventy-two course sections that involved a computing component. Enrollments in these classes totalled 998, including 603 individual students or approximately 60 percent of the student body. An additional eighty-six students not enrolled in any course involving computing used the Academic Computing Center to prepare papers, complete papers, prepare student organization materials, and print resumes. This brings the total number of students who used computing in 1986–87 close to 70 percent of the student body. At least ninety-two faculty members (60 percent of all faculty) representing every academic department on campus are using computing for research, department administration, classroom preparation, and/or professional publication. Since 1985, the college has offered a no-interest loan plan and a discount purchasing plan as part of a partnership with Apple Computer, to provide a means for users to share the costs with the college to reach the level of access desired by both faculty and students.

Since 1977, the college library has participated in the Research Libraries Information Network (RLIN), used for the acquisition and cataloging of the materials added to Mills' collection. In 1987, the library began using the Midwest Technical Services System for the procurement and accounting functions in the acquisitions process. Mills also offers searches of the DIALOG database, with the library currently paying the cost for advanced student searches and faculty paying with grant funds when available.

The college library's automation plan, devised in 1986, involves four stages. The first is the construction of the all-new F. W. Olin Library as an electronic library with personal computer work areas, and wiring and conduits for future campuswide network access. Construction will start in the summer of 1988 with completion anticipated in the fall of 1989. The second stage is the conversion into machine-readable form of the records for all pre-1977 acquisitions which are not on the RLIN database. The merging of RLIN records with the pre-1977 entries will provide a database of the library's full collection. Records conversion will proceed in parallel with construction of the F. W. Olin Library. The third stage is the selection and implementation of the integrated library system, which will combine all major library functions, including the online public catalog and circulation. Our goal is to have the integrated system in place approximately two years after the new library is completed. The fourth stage requires the installation of the campus communications network, to provide faculty, students and staff remote access to the online catalog.

In 1984-85, the Educational Technology Research Committee (ETRC) was created to assist in planning for future academic improvements at Mills based on new technology. The committee created a two-part plan to expand the use of microcomputers in the college's academic division as a supplement to the use of the VAX minicomputer. Local area networks (LANs) of Macintoshes sharing LaserWriters and hard disks using AppleTalk are now located in the Computer Learning Studio Faculty Training Center, the Academic Computer Center, the Computer Learning Studio Sales Center, the Provost's office, the Department of Physical Science, and the Audio-Visual Technical Services Office. Additional LANs are planned this year in the Interdisciplinary Computer Science Lab, the English Writing Lab, and the Center for Contemporary Music. An experimental Ethernet network allowing our VAX to serve as a file server to Macintosh users will be installed in March. The ETRC committee and the college have turned their attention to the broader problems posed by the urgent need for an integrated system that will combine improved voice communication by telephone with data transmission and video capabilities. A consultant reviewed our communications system. His very strong recommendation is that Mills purchase a comprehensive new system to replace our inadequate current cabling. At this point, we are working with a telecommunications expert who is familiar with the higher education environment to help us decide precisely what kind of system to purchase.

The goal of our planning process is to develop a program that will address the college's needs for communication systems to support academic and administrative activities for at least the next five-to-seven years. The plan must take into account needs for different forms of communication (voice, data, video), current and future visions for the computing environment on the Mills campus, current and projected demands (including service to future buildings), and the physical, finanacial, and operational constraints of the college. The resulting system should promote improved communications throughout the community through electronic mail, electronic document transfers, electronic library catalog access, and resource sharing; enhance student skills in learning to make informed judgments and decisions from an ever-increasing flow of information available in each discipline; and increase access to computer resources with growth in the numbers of personal computers and workstations. The communications plan must be consistent with academic, administrative, and library computing plans and technically integrated with them, as well as with overall capital investment and budget strategy for the combined technologies.

The long-term goals the college has set for a campuswide communications system include:

1. Stressing the development of a user community centered on the new campus communication system.

2. Creating a basic communication network linking all buildings that provides for voice and data communication as well as the future potential for video transmission.

3. Providing every full-time faculty member and each administrative office with a workstation that connects with the campus network for electronic communication.

4. Planning for the eventual introduction of similar workstations in student residence rooms, with the college providing the communication link and the student providing the workstation.

5. Providing decentralized access in individual academic buildings to essential audiovisual tools.

6. Integrating staff support available to faculty, students, and staff in using computers, electronic communications, and audiovisual devices.

Mississippi College

Mississippi College is a private, church-related, coeducational institution of liberal arts and sciences and professional studies. With a faculty of 207 and a student enrollment of 3,448, the college endeavors to offers a broadly based liberal arts undergraduate program and several comprehensive programs administered by Schools of Business, Education, Graduate Studies, Nursing, and Law.

The college provides a computer laboratory utilized primarily by students formally enrolled in computing science courses. The laboratory contains a network of five IBM microcomputers with an IBM XT as the driver. Also available in the laboratory are three IBM PC System II/Model 50 computers with hard disk drives for use by both students and faculty. Eighteen additional stations in the laboratory are equipped with HP terminals which provide student access to the Hewlett Packard 3000 minicomputer used exclusively for academic computing. A new classroom furnished with twenty-four IBM microcomputers System II/Model 30, and supporting printers, opened in fall 1987 for campuswide use in teaching. Several academic departments have made personal computers available in faculty offices to promote and enhance faculty applications of computer-aided instruction (CAI). To further assist and encourage faculty and staff to use computers, faculty members of the Computing Science Department and the School of Business have conducted comprehensive workshops in the introduction and use of computers and CAI.

Library automation consists of the limited use of computers by the library staff. The library is a member of SOLINET (Southeastern Library Network) and this provides access to more than 15 million bibliographic records of the national OCLC database. The Mississippi College Library also uses DIALOG.

Academic computing does not at present involve campus networking.

Plans for expansion or development of academic computing include providing an additional computer-equipped classroom for campuswide instruction use to open in the fall of 1988, continuing an education program for college faculty and staff in the use of computers, encouraging further automation of the Library/Media Center, and investigating the need for and feasibility of campuswide networking.

Occidental College

Occidental College is an independent liberal arts college with an enrollment of 1,689 students, of whom 1,664 are undergraduates and 37 are enrolled in international or off-campus programs. The full-time faculty numbers 118. An additional 50 adjuncts bring the actual total instructional staff to 166, for an FTE of 135.

At present, our academic computing environment consists of a network of PRIME computers with 130 terminals, 150 personal computers, and a number of specialized machines in science and social science labs. We have student PC and terminal labs in several buildings and a central open access lab in the library with forty terminals and eighteen personal computers. We have four FTE staff members plus a number of student employees devoted to the support of academic computing.

During the past several years the Mary Norton Clapp Library has been developing plans to automate. Acquisitions since 1978 have been cataloged in machine-readable form through the OCLC system. A consultant was hired in 1985 to develop a feasibility report. A needs analysis was done resulting in a functional study of library operations emphasizing those aspects directly affected by automation. An automation proposal has been developed that includes preparation and implementation plans. We have recently hired another automation consultant and have begun working on the development of an RFP for both system purchase and retrospective conversion of books, serials, and government documents. This plan should be completed by the end of February. Occidental's library has been doing DIALOG searches for over three years, and has recently introduced the Infotrac System and the OCLC Interlibrary Loan Subsystem for resource sharing.

Our present campus network consists of a proprietary local area network connecting our campus mainframe along with hardwired connections between most microcomputers and the mainframe network. We have connected our campus electronic mail system to the national networks (via a UUCP link to Caltech) and the sophistication of the mail systems involved gives us easy and fast mail service to/from the standard national networks (ARPANET, BITNET, and CSNET). The college is in the process of registering as a domain to facilitate the addressing of Occidental users by members of BITNET.

We hope to go forward with library automation in the coming year. Meanwhile, we will continue to improve our academic systems. We are presently adding a network of Sun workstations in the physics department and our art department is installing an innovative cataloging system for its extensive collection of art slides. We are now installing in the library two Wilsondisc workstations for students to search humanities and social science indices. The turnkey system we envision purchasing will include an online public access catalog, circulation and reserves, acquisitions, serials control and cataloging authority. This system will have the capability to link with other campus computing terminals in a manner transparent to the user through a local area network and should be implemented by January 1989. Local area networks and possible connections between our present academic computing resources and the proposed library system are currently under active consideration.

Reed College

Reed College is a private, nonsectarian institution of liberal arts and sciences. The college has an enrollment of 1,250 students, a faculty of 120, and a staff of 180.

In 1983, the faculty and trustees of Reed College adopted the *Five-Year Master Plan for Computing Resources at Reed College*. The goal of the *Master Plan* is to integrate computing technology into the academic life of the college across all disciplines. We are well on our way to accomplishing that goal. Faculty now use their personal computers, laserwriters, mainframe capability, and hard disk storage to write, conduct research, prepare course materials, make complex calculations, and develop new academic software. Students use Macintosh personal computers and printers, networked with a DEC VAX 11/785 mainframe computer, for text processing, mainframe communications, statistical analysis, graphics production, computer exploration, and electronic mail to search remote databases and communicate with scholars around the world. Reed is an important developer of academic software for research in chemistry, human physiology, neural biology, psychology, and physics, and supplies special technology to industry. More than 130 educational institutions, private laboratories, and industries use Reed-developed software or technology. Reed College is a member of the Apple University Consortium.

During this 1987–88 academic year, our research staff will continue to identify and study courseware problems, develop network software, design and program courseware, and develop guidelines for further research and development. We plan to upgrade the student computer laboratories (Information Resources Centers, or IRCs) and departmental networks, and purchase laboratory hardware and software to provide state-of-the-art academic courseware for our faculty and students. We will also continue to provide support staff to assist faculty and students in the use of software and hardware.

Through the integrated library computer system project, Reed is automating the library catalog and circulation information. The campus network provides students and faculty with access to the online library catalog from all academic buildings.

The library staff has converted 93 percent of the library's records to machine-readable form. Retrospective conversion should be completed within a year. The test period with the Carlyle TOMUS online catalog ended October 1986, with overwhelming acceptance by the community. Software for circulation will be installed as soon as it is available from Carlyle. Acquisitions and serials operations are currently supported by software developed by Reed staff.

The Reed College network consists of a fiber-optic Ethernet backbone that connects all academic buildings. Within each building, AppleTalk is used to connect Macintoshes to departmental laserwriters and file servers. The AppleTalk networks are connected to the Ethernet using Kinetics AppleTalk Ethernet Gateways. These provide access to the VAX, library computer system, and AppleTalk services located on other AppleTalk networks. Other personal computers and workstations are connected to the network using terminal servers or direct connection to the Ethernet.

We plan to connect residence halls during the 1988-89 academic year if funding becomes available. Current networking projects include providing Macintosh file service from Unix hosts such as the VAX, providing better access to national networks such as BITNET, providing access to AppleTalk services from off campus, and providing an easy-to-use electronic mail system for the campus.

Sonoma State University

The instructional programs of Sonoma State University are grounded in the liberal arts and sciences. The university enrolls approximately 6,100 students (4,600 FTE) and is allocated about 265 faculty positions.

Academic computing at Sonoma State includes both shared systems and stand-alone systems. The shared systems include a CYBER 170-730 mainframe with numerous language compilers, statistical packages, and databases; a CYBER 180-830 mainframe used primarily for administrative applications with an EDEN student records system for academic advisement; two PRIME 9755 minicomputers with language compilers, UNIX simulation, statistical packages, databases, text editing, business applications, and limited graphics; four self-instructional labs, one of which is located in the library, with approximately 100 terminals for student access to the system described; and numerous terminals and departmental and faculty offices.

The stand-alone systems include four self-instruction microcomputer labs (IBM PC/XT, Apple IIe, Macintosh Plus, and Macintosh II) that are heavily used by nearly all of the disciplines represented on campus; and numerous microcomputers in discipline-based instructional labs (for instance, physics, geography, and psychology) and limited numbers of systems in faculty and departmental offices.

Little use is made of newer technologies such as CD-ROM, interactive video disks, or course-authoring systems for academic computing purposes.

The library provides its users with CL Systems Inc. (CLSI), an automated circulation system maintained on a DEC PDP 11 minicomputer with dial-up access. Theoretically, the system could be used as a partial online catalog, but this capacity has not been explored. The library also provides CD-ROM access to the ERIC database for education and Infotrak, an information database for periodical literature which is run on a dedicated microcomputer. Access to online databases is provided through DIALOG and interlibrary loan is facilitated through the use of the OCLC Interlibrary Loan Subsystem and OnTyme electronic mail service.

Additionally, most cataloging is done using the OCLC system. An online public access catalog is planned for implementation, as part of a CSU-wide effort in 1989. At that time, it is hoped that automated acquisitions and serials check-in will also be acquired. The library is also investigating the use of microcomputer-based systems for these activities and for bibliographic database file development. It is expected that more CD-ROM and interactive disc systems will be purchased within the year.

Nearly all of the computing facilities on campus are linked to one another via a central data PBX. A new telephone PBX installed in June 1987 provides additional capability for voice and data switching. The bandwidth of present facilities is limited and will probably prove unable to meet demands within three to four years.

A Campus Information Resources Planning Committee was inaugurated this year to plan an integrated information system. Within the next few years, the university expects to install an Online Public Access Catalog system and a campuswide data network, replace its shared computing facilities, and increase the number of workstations in all areas of academic computing. Faculty workshops on newer technologies are also planned during the next year.

About the Authors

William O. Beeman is Associate Director for Program Analysis at the Institute for Research in Information and Scholarship (IRIS) and Associate Professor of Anthropology at Brown University. His past research has centered on linguistic anthropology, culture and cognition, applied anthropology and the social aspects of computing in contemporary society. Some of his recent monographs and articles include "The Future of Campus Computerization," "Computers and Human Consciousness," *Object, Image and Inquiry: The Art Historian at Work,* and *Intermedia: A Case Study of Innovation in Higher Education.*

Richard W. Boss, Senior Management Consultant at Information Systems Consultants, Inc., of Washington D. C., has seventeen years of administrative experience in research libraries and has completed over 300 consulting assignments in the areas of library and information science technology, management, and facilities planning. His clients have included academic, national, public, school, and special libraries; library consortia; museums; and Fortune 500 companies. Mr. Boss has degrees in library science and political science, and is the author of numerous monographs and articles.

Richard A. Detweiler is Associate Vice President for Planning and Communication and Professor of Psychology at Drew University. He was responsible for Drew University's Computer Initiative in 1983 – 85, in which he designed, implemented, and managed a program to integrate personal computers into a liberal arts curriculum. In his current position, he is responsible for short- and long-term programmatic and administrative planning and implementation and for all technology-related operations of the university. Mr. Detweiler holds a Ph.D. from Princeton in social psychology. His chief research interest is in the psychology of international and intercultural affairs.

Evan Ira Farber has been College Librarian of Earlham College since 1962. His undergraduate and professional degrees are from the University of North Carolina; he also has a D.H.L. from St. Lawrence University. He has taught at several library schools and is the author of numerous books and articles, in addition to serving as a consultant on more than 100 college campuses. He was president of the Association of College and Research Libraries in 1979/80, and was selected National Academic/ Research Librarian of the Year. He is widely known for his emphatic insistence—and its success at Earlham—that the library constitute an integral part of the teaching and learning process of undergraduate education.

James W. Johnson, Vice President for Computing at the University of Houston, is one of the highest ranking computing officers in American higher education. As one of the university's four vice presidents, he is involved in overall university policy setting as well as the planning and implementation of the computer intensive environment, with direct authority for academic computing, administrative computing, and communication systems. Before joining the University of Houston in 1985, Mr. Johnson held several faculty and administrative positions at the University of Iowa. Mr. Johnson earned his A.B. in economics from Knox College and his M.B.A. at the University of Illinois.

Daphne N. Layton, formerly Assistant Director of Programs at the Association of American Colleges, designed and organized the series of regional conferences at which these papers were presented. As a member of the AAC staff from 1984 to 1987, Ms. Layton was responsible for several association programs. She now [1987] works for the Commission on the Future of the University at the University of Massachusetts and will begin a doctoral program in Administration, Planning, and Social Policy at the Harvard Graduate School of Education in fall 1988. Ms. Layton has a B.A. in music from Yale University.

Patricia C. Skarulis is Vice President for Information Systems at Duke University. She holds a B.A. and an M.A. in mathematics from St. John's University, and attended the Institute for Educational Management at Harvard University. Before coming to Duke in 1983, she served in various administrative capacities related to computing at Princeton, Rutgers, and Bowdoin. She has been professionally active in a number of organizations, including the Society for Information Management, CAUSE, NCHEMS, and EDUCOM.